Strategic Change and Transformation

Strategic change and transformation are words used very commonly in business parlance but rarely defined. Besides, change and transformations are often used interchangeably. Thus the correct perspective of viewing change and transformations is missing from management literature. How is change different from transformation? Do all changes lead to renewal? What are the characteristics of strategic changes?

This book re-addresses some of our current assumptions and understanding of change and transformation when viewed through both academic and business lenses. It is a balanced and well-rounded perspective on how strategic change and transformation can be brought about successfully in organizations specifically with the perspective from an emerging economy like India.

Swarup Kumar Dutta is an Assistant Professor in the Strategic Management Area at Indian Institute of Management, Ranchi, India.

Routledge Focus on Management and Society

Series Editor: **Anindya Sen**, Professor of Economics, Indian Institute of Management Calcutta, Kolkata, West Bengal, India

The Focus series is designed to introduce management theorists and researchers (as well as the lay public) to a diverse set of topics relevant directly or peripherally to management in a concise format, without sacrificing basic rigor. The invisible hand of market has today been replaced by the visible hand of managerial capitalism. As the power and role of the managers expanded, the world also became more dynamic and volatile. To run their organizations more efficiently, the managers need to be aware of new developments taking place all around them. The Focus series addresses this need by presenting a number of short volumes which deal with important managerial issues in the Indian context. Volumes planned for the series will not only cover topics which are of perennial interest to managers, but also emerging areas of interest like neuro-marketing. Some of the well-established areas of research like bottom-of-the-pyramid marketing will be dealt with specifically in the Indian context as well as critical developments in other fields, like auction theory.

Strategic Change and Transformation
Managing Renewal in Organizations
Swarup Kumar Dutta

Poor Marketing
Insights from Marketing to the Poor
Ramendra Singh

Neuromarketing in India
Understanding the Indian Consumer
Tanusree Dutta and Manas Kumar Mandal

Strategic Change and Transformation

Managing Renewal in Organizations

Swarup Kumar Dutta

LONDON AND NEW YORK

First published in paperback 2024

First published 2019
by Routledge
4 Park Square, Milton Park, Abingdon, Oxon OX14 4RN

and by Routledge
605 Third Avenue, New York, NY 10158

Routledge is an imprint of the Taylor & Francis Group, an informa business

© 2019, 2024 Swarup Kumar Dutta

Publisher's Note
The publisher has gone to great lengths to ensure the quality of this reprint but points out that some imperfections in the original copies may be apparent.

British Library Cataloguing-in-Publication Data
A catalogue record for this book is available from the British Library

Library of Congress Cataloging-in-Publication Data
Names: Dutta, Swarup Kumar, author.
Title: Strategic change and transformation: managing renewal
in organizations / Swarup Kumar Dutta.
Description: First Edition. | New York: Routledge, 2019. |
Includes bibliographical references and index.
Identifiers: LCCN 2018022708 | ISBN 9781138576704 (hardback) |
ISBN 9781351269247 (ebook)
Subjects: LCSH: Organizational change. | Strategic planning.
Classification: LCC HD58.8. D88 2019 | DDC 658.4/06–dc23
LC record available at https://lccn.loc.gov/2018022708

ISBN: 978-1-03-293120-3 (pbk)
ISBN: 978-1-138-57670-4 (hbk)
ISBN: 978-1-351-26924-7 (ebk)

DOI: 10.4324/9781351269247

Typeset in Times New Roman
by Out of House Publishing

Contents

Illustrations

Figures

Tables

Preface

The idea of change in organizations is a very complex one. Having been a practicing manager first, I had observed and been a part of a few change initiatives in organizations. Thereafter as an academic, I had read about many changes and renewal happening in companies. Also the idea of Indian companies undergoing radical change as reported by Sumantra Ghoshal has deeply intrigued me and made me study companies which resulted in a few case studies. All these strands when put together made me realize that it is tempting to write a book to understand the change initiatives a little better in organizations.

This book is an attempt to understand strategic change and transformation in companies in a more detailed way looking at the strategic aspects of change. Often change management is understood to be just a process, however looking at the landscape of different industries, change management is more than just a process and often entails the context, content and the outcome.

This book in a way attempts to highlight and shed light on the major dimensions of strategic change and renewal in organizations.

Acknowledgments

The writings of the late management guru, Prof. Sumantra Ghoshal have deeply inspired me in understanding how companies manage change and bring about renewal in companies. Also, the support of Prof. Constance Helfat while I was pursuing my Ph.D. have helped me in having an all-round view. My sincere thanks to Prof. C. Gopalakrishnan for his unwavering attention in understanding phenomena, which has helped me in great detail.

My sincere thanks to Prof. A. Sen for constantly supporting and guiding me in writing this book. Last but not least my thanks to the Faculty Members at Indian Institute of Management, Ranchi, India for their continuous encouragement.

1 Introduction to *Strategic Change and Transformation*

1.1 How organizations cope with changing environments

Most of the research efforts in strategic management are rooted in studies of how firms can stabilize themselves and not on how to adjust to the changes in the external environment. There has been relatively less focus on how multi-unit firms develop firm-specific capabilities and how they renew them to shifts in the industry. How firms change and adjust to environmental shocks has been studied by organizational theorists like Barnard in *Functions of the executive* (1938), and Pettigrew in *The awakening giant* (1985) and the tradition has continued wherein the process of change in organizations has been studied. But from the perspectives of how organizations were renewed, the organization theory writers focused on the process of change and were rarely interested about the content of change.

Thus from the position of why firms exist, the inherent tensions of the change process, particularly the tension between change and stability, need to be analyzed along with the content and outcome of change.

The underlying lesson is simple yet unknown to many firms. Sustained performance of firms is based on the capabilities to manage the balance between two conflicting objectives: the need for ongoing improvement in leveraging existing skills and competencies through constant exploitation and the need for new growth opportunities through constant exploration. This is done by continuous renewal and revitalization of strategy, organization and people.

There is nothing new about these words but most managers see the processes of exploitation and exploration as mutually exclusive. Most companies are focused on improving their current market offerings and on stability in the current operating environment. As a result, many a time the focus is on short-term wins rather than trying to position the firm in the future in the ever-changing environmental landscape.

1.2 Change versus transformation

Not all companies need transformation. In the context of changing business and technological landscapes, most companies must have the capacity to evolve and change. Typically for a change to get effected, a company should alter or realign some aspect of their strategy, organization or culture, while retaining others. This is normally referred to as change.

Transformation in contrast is the systematic, simultaneous and deliberate attack across many fronts that fundamentally alters the basic rhythm and character of a company. In India companies like L&T, Ceat Tyres, Bajaj Auto, Eveready Industries, etc. have gone through a transformation process but many companies have not. A number of companies like Hero Motors (erstwhile Hero Honda Motors Ltd) did not have to go through major transformation and have been successful by effecting some amount of strategic changes.

1.3 Dealing with the paradoxes

The problem of change in organizations is a relative one; as many have pointed out (like Bate in *Strategies for cultural change* (1994)), organizations are always in a dynamic mode of change, but the speed of change may be insufficient or too slow, largely where competition is hypercompetitive in nature or when firms face technological shifts. Competition threatens survival if the pace of change is too slow. But adjustment to competition is also risky; change may fail or firms may over react, leading to even more serious consequences. Thus organizations that wish to adjust need to reconcile the paradox of conflicting forces for change and stability. The pressure to change comes not just from the threats to survival but also from the desire to grow and be more successful. Resolving the paradox of change and preservation means recognizing that continuous renewal inside a complex firm is far from easy. Abrupt changes where the scope of change is large can lead to chaos and confusion, sending conflicting signals about change of organizational culture and many a time lead to further organizational crisis. While in the short term organizations that are chaotic survive, in the long run, they are likely to collapse. Thus firms need control mechanisms that prevent the fissuring. Major emphasis has been placed on two important mechanisms that separate the change and stability either by time or by place.

In spatial separation, one part of the organization is responsible for undertaking the process of change and renewal while the other parts remain unaffected. Several researchers have opined that in a spatial separation process of change, a specialist research and development group is involved. More often, there is a self-appointed function such as marketing or production that is seen as the spearhead of new ideas. In multidivisional organizations, usually the senior level team acts as the change agent. In general, in spatial separation the groups that are changing and the groups that are stable are both not insulated from change, for effective realignment calls for harnessing ideas generated by the dynamic sections to be carried over into the rest of the organization.

The other method of resolving the dilemma is to have the whole organization alternating between periods of stability and periods of change. Such changes are most apparent in organizations experiencing major change programs such as turnarounds. The detail of temporal change usually shows some spatial adjustment as well. For example, top management may be in a state of change while other parts are stable, and then the baton is handed down to the next level for it to change while top management regains some sense of stability. Looking at it holistically, there are clear cycles of "unfreeze, move and refreeze" that often get repeated.

These possibilities of resolving the dilemma of stability and change have been quite general and focused on broad categories of processes. Thus the important difference between the two mechanisms is the approach to speed and risk. The method of spatial separation of change and stability allows the organization to experiment in one place while keeping the other part constant. This method of managing change appears to be one of risk control, for some of the dangers of failure are contained simultaneously, thereby allowing variety to increase which helps in widening the risk spread. Thus speed of change is sacrificed. Temporal separation allows the whole organization to adjust to sharp and sudden shocks more holistically and quickly. Under temporal separation, the possibilities of failure may be greater if the change process loses control. Moreover, variety is not increased but the speed of execution may be faster. The mechanism of spatial separation will be most effective where the organization needs to contain the risks of change and is not concerned with speedy reaction to outside events. In contrast, a temporal separation will be more effective where there is a pressing urgency for the whole organization to respond collectively.

How Kodak failed

There are few corporate blunders as staggering as Kodak's missed opportunities in digital photography, a technology that it invented. This strategic failure was the direct cause of Kodak's decades-long decline as digital photography destroyed its film-based business model.

A book by former Kodak executive offers insight on the choices that set Kodak on the path to bankruptcy. Barabba's book, *The decision loom: A design for interactive decision-making in organizations* (2011), also offers sage advice on how other organizations grappling with disruptive technologies might avoid their own Kodak moments.

Steve Sasson, the Kodak engineer who invented the first digital camera in 1975, characterized the initial corporate response to his invention this way: But it was filmless photography, so management's reaction was, "that's cute—but don't tell anyone about it."

Kodak management's inability to see digital photography as a disruptive technology, even as its researchers extended the boundaries of the technology, would continue for decades. As late as 2007, a Kodak marketing video felt the need to trumpet that "Kodak is back" and that Kodak "wasn't going to play grab ass anymore" with digital.

To understand how Kodak could stay in denial for so long, Vince Barabba starts the story from 1981, when he was Kodak's head of market intelligence. Around the time that Sony introduced the first electronic camera, one of Kodak's largest retailer photo finishers asked him whether they should be concerned about digital photography. With the support of Kodak's CEO, Barabba conducted a very extensive research effort that looked at the core technologies and likely adoption curves around silver halide film versus digital photography. The results of the study produced both "bad" and "good" news. The "bad" news was that digital photography had the potential capability to replace Kodak's established film-based business. The "good" news was that it would take some time for that to occur and that Kodak had roughly ten years to prepare for the transition.

The study's projections were based on numerous factors, including: the cost of digital photography equipment; the quality of images and prints; and the interoperability of various components, such as cameras, displays and printers. All pointed to the conclusion that adoption of digital photography would be minimal and non-threatening for a time. History proved the study's conclusions to be remarkably accurate, both in the short and long term. The problem is that during its ten-year window of opportunity, Kodak did little to prepare for the later disruption. In fact, Kodak made exactly the mistake that George Eastman, its founder, avoided twice before, when he gave up a profitable dry-plate business to move to film and when he invested in color film even though it was demonstrably inferior to black and white film (which Kodak dominated).

Barabba left Kodak in 1985 but remained close to its senior management. Thus he got a close look at the fact that, rather than prepare for the time when digital photography would replace film, as Eastman had with prior disruptive technologies, Kodak choose to use digital to improve the quality of film. This strategy continued even though, in 1986, Kodak's research labs developed the first mega-pixel camera, one of the milestones that Barabba's study had forecasted as a tipping point in terms of the viability of standalone digital photography.

In *Billion-dollar lessons: What you can learn from the most inexcusable business failures of the last 25 years* (Carroll & Mui, 2008), it is pointed out that Kodak also suffered several other significant, self-inflicted wounds in those pivotal years. In 1989, the Kodak board of directors had a chance to make a course change when Colby Chandler, the CEO, retired. The choices came down to Phil Samper and Kay R. Whitmore. Whitmore represented the traditional film business, where he had moved up the ranks for three decades. Samper had a deep appreciation for digital technology. The board chose Whitmore. As the *New York Times* reported at the time, Mr. Whitmore said he would make sure Kodak stayed closer to its core businesses in film and photographic chemicals.

For more than another decade, a series of new Kodak CEOs would bemoan his predecessor's failure to transform the organization to digital, declare his own intention to do so and proceed to fail at the transition as well. George Fisher, who was lured from his position as CEO of Motorola to succeed Whitmore in 1993, captured the core issue when he told the *New York Times* that Kodak regarded digital photography as the enemy, an evil juggernaut that would kill the chemical-based film and paper business that had fueled Kodak's sales and profits for decades.

Addressing strategic decision-making quandaries such as those faced by Kodak is one of the prime questions addressed in Vince

Barabba's book, *The decision loom*. Kodak management not only presided over the creation of technological breakthroughs but was also presented with an accurate market assessment about the risks and opportunities of such capabilities. Yet Kodak failed in making the right strategic choices.

Barabba argues that four interrelated capabilities are necessary to enable effective enterprise-wide decision-making—none of which were particularly well represented during pivotal decisions at Kodak:

1. Having an enterprise mindset that is open to change. Unless those at the top are sufficiently open and willing to consider all options, the decision-making process soon gets distorted. Unlike its founder, George Eastman, who twice adopted disruptive photographic technology, Kodak's management in the 1980s and 1990s were unwilling to consider digital as a replacement for film. This limited them to a fundamentally flawed path.

2. Thinking and acting holistically. Separating out and then optimizing different functions usually reduces the effectiveness of the whole. In Kodak's case, management did a reasonable job of understanding how the parts of the enterprise (including its photo finishing partners) interacted within the framework of the existing technology. There was, however, little appreciation for the effort being conducted in the Kodak Research Labs with digital technology.

3. Being able to adapt the business design to changing conditions. Barabba offers three different business designs along a mechanistic to organismic continuum—make-and-sell, sense-and-respond and anticipate-and-lead. The right design depends on the predictability of the market. Kodak's unwillingness to change its large and highly efficient ability to make-and-sell film in the face of developing digital technologies lost it the chance to adopt an anticipate-and-lead design that could have secured it a leading position in digital image processing.

4. Making decisions interactively using a variety of methods. This refers to the ability to incorporate a range of sophisticated decision support tools when tackling complex business problems. Kodak had a very effective decision support process in place but failed to use that information effectively.

While *The decision loom* goes a long way to explaining Kodak's slow reaction to digital photography, its real value is as a guidepost for today's managers dealing with ever-more disruptive changes. Given that there are few industries not grappling with disruptive change, it is a valuable book for any senior (or aspiring) manager to read.

Critical integration

While Kodak did make efforts to outsource its camera manufacturing (and thus fill some gaps in expertise), the outsourcing arrangement did not achieve the integration of external knowledge with Kodak's own internal knowledge that was so critical to continued innovation. As a result, Kodak remained stuck in the lower end of the digital camera spectrum and could never compete in the high end of the spectrum, which is where the bulk of the profits are.

So what lessons do Kodak's problems hold for others?

The key stumbling block was its inability to convert its technical expertise into tangible products that could be sold profitably (in other words a sustainable business model). Kodak had several gaps in its expertise to design a complete business model but lacked the clarity of vision or the continuity of leadership to acquire the resources in a systematic fashion, let alone integrate them with its considerable internal knowledge of digital imaging. Other companies facing similar technological discontinuities would do well to remember the critical role of integration of internal and external knowledge to achieve innovation, which would, in turn, improve their chances of successful adaptation.

1. Source: www.forbes.com/sites/chunkamui/2012/01/18/how-kodak-failed/#21cc94206f27
2. http://thinkbusiness.nus.edu/article/kodak/ accessed on August 20, 2017

References

Barabba, V. P. (2011). *The decision loom: A design for interactive decision-making in organizations.* Axminster: Triarchy Press.

Barnard, C. I. (1938). *The functions of the executive.* Cambridge, MA: Harvard University Press.

Bate, P. (1994). *Strategies for cultural change.* Oxford. Butterworth Heinemann.

Carroll, P. B., & Mui, C. (2008). *Billion-dollar lessons: What you can learn from the most inexcusable business failures of the last 25 years.* New York, NY: Portfolio.

Pettigrew, A. M. (1985). *The awakening giant.* Oxford: Blackwell.

2 Strategic renewal in organizations

2.1 Strategic change and renewal

In its broadest definition, change means to make or become different. Thus change can be understood as refreshing or replacing any attributes, but it need not create renewal. For example, change can be referred to indicate any extensions of products or services. For that matter any form of adding or removing an element can be referred to as change.

Thus based on the above discussion, many a time strategic renewal is understood to be strategic change and hence both these terms are used loosely. On a more general note, strategic renewal is frequently used to explain examples of strategic change with most examples highlighting the process of change; however, strategic renewal is something more than the process of change. There are important content aspects as well to strategic renewal. To define the term "strategic renewal," we need to look at each of the words carefully.

Strategic. Numerous ways to define "strategy," and also several conceptions of what "strategic" is all about, have been proposed. Strategic is understood as "that which relates to the long-term prospects of the company and has a critical influence on its success or failure." Thus any attribute is strategic in nature if the firm's future prospects are related to it in a significant way. The lists of potential factors that fall into the category as critical to an organization's future could be goals, products, services, policies, the firm's ability to compete in product markets I rivals, business scope, structure and administrative systems. Critical intangible and tangible resources, capabilities, routines and people that have the ability to affect the firm's future are also strategic in nature.

Renewal. The term "renew" is understood as "to make like new." Synonyms include "to refresh" or "to revitalize" by restoring strength or animation. Renewal is then one type of change, indicating all forms of renewal are changes but not all changes are renewal in nature.

2.2 What constitutes strategic renewal

What constitutes "refreshment" or "replacement" for an organization needs to be further understood.

1. Refreshment or replacement does not imply restoration of an attribute to its original state. For example, a firm can substitute one type of attribute with a totally different attribute.
2. Refreshment or replacement can be in part or complete. Also firms can decide not to replace an attribute in its present form if the intended purpose is served.
3. Refreshment or replacement may extend beyond the original attribute in either size or scope of application.
4. Firms can undertake strategic refreshment through reconfiguration of presently available attributes, with or without modifications.
5. Firms may undertake strategic renewal to refresh or replace current organizational attributes that serve a useful function in the short term, but chances are that it may not do so in the long term.
6. Finally, strategic renewal often connotes momentum. The verb "regrow" basically means to continue the growth path after any interruption.

Strategic renewal further signifies the combination of process, content and outcomes of change. As an example the process of renewal in a firm can be a change management program, the content of change can be knowledge management and the outcome can be development of superior competitive advantages to compete effectively in the market place.

2.3 Characteristics and types of renewal

Characteristics

a) Strategic renewal relates to that which has the potential to substantially affect the long-term prospects of a company.
b) Strategic renewal is a combination of the process, content and outcome of refreshment or replacement.
c) Strategic renewal involves the refreshment or replacement of attributes of an organization (Agarwal & Helfat, 2009).

d) Such refreshment or replacement aims to provide a foundation for future growth or development.

Thus any act of refreshment or replacement of attributes like the process, content or outcome that can significantly affect the long-term prospects of a firm is understood to be strategic renewal.

Types of strategic renewal

The classification of firms based on mechanisms of renewal and accordingly can be classified as: (i) discontinuous renewal; and (ii) incremental (continual) renewal.

Discontinuous transformations. If we see the history of transformation studies of companies, the majority of the studies have focused their attention on analyses of discontinuous transformations. Major changes such as a new technology that makes the existing technology obsolete or shifting customer demand may cause a company to fundamentally alter one or more aspects of its strategy and organization which are basically discontinuous transformations. Discontinuous transformations involve replacing important parts of a company and its strategy, and affect the long-term prospects of the firm. Thus, major transformations involve change along multiple dimensions, such as business model changes, changes in technological base, organizational structural mechanisms, resources, routines, capabilities and organizational mindset all of which entail strategic renewal.

Continual (incremental) transformations. As major transformations can pose great difficulties due to the extent of change required, many companies find it very hard to effect such major changes and instead may seek to continuously renew themselves in incremental ways periodically in the hope of keeping pace with and even leading, external environment changes. This track of managing transformations is in line with researches on ambidexterity which focus on ways in which firms can build new businesses while operating matured businesses. These are typically incremental strategic renewal efforts.

If proactive renewal efforts are taken on an incremental basis it may generate for firms better ways of making adjustments with changes in the external environment. These efforts will go a long way in preparing the organization for a difficult transformation in future. As an example Boeing undertook a fusion of related innovations and a sequence of path-dependent opportunities in pursuit of persistent advantage.

Examples of incremental renewal can include experimentation at the periphery outside the core business such as through corporate venturing, or it can include incremental modifications to the core businesses of the company. For instance, Johnson and Johnson's history exemplifies the purposeful experimentation through acquisitions and subsequent reconfiguration of divisions and products. Incremental strategic renewal may even enable the firm to shape the external environment to its advantage. For example, by proactively introducing new generations of personal computer (PC) chips on a regular basis, Intel created a barrier to new entry that enabled the firm to dominate its industry for years. As the examples of Johnson and Johnson and Intel indicate, not all incremental renewal occurs in response to a previous change in the external environment.

2.4 How organizations can stay ahead by periodic strategic renewal

Firms conduct many activities on a regular basis that may facilitate renewal, outside of research and development (R&D), with accompanying opportunities for cumulative innovation. Conducting renewal activities such as R&D on a regular basis requires underlying processes, rules, routines and resources, along with the capabilities to develop and execute such activities, including dynamic capabilities. Thus, dynamic capabilities can play a significant role in strategic renewal through modification and reconfiguration of the organization's resource base. Given the potential benefits of continual efforts directed at strategic renewal, questions may arise as to why firms attempt major transformations. One answer might be that some changes in the external environment are difficult to anticipate. Another answer might be that continuous adaptation may be hard for organizations to manage effectively, because this may conflict with routines that enable companies to perform current tasks well.

One solution to this tension between routines and change is to institutionalize continuous renewal through routines, and organizational structure e.g. dedicated organizational units in charge of specific types of renewal activities such as alliances and incentives to conduct ongoing renewal activities. Besides, if a firm develops capabilities which are dynamic in nature and the application of the same is used specifically as an institutional mechanism to drive renewal, the effectiveness of the renewal process will be highly enhanced, e.g. GE has a template for managing acquisitions worldwide which acts as a template for making and integrating acquisitions. Thus both continuous strategic renewal and discontinuous transformations offer pathways for firms to make transformations by which the end state of the firm after transformation differs from the state when the transformation started. A series of small incremental changes can manifest into a wide impacting change when visualized over a relatively longer time period. This is precisely why both forms of the mentioned transformations are effective mechanisms for making strategic changes in companies.

Strategic renewal applies not only to mature firms, but also to young firms. If we look at the history of Intel, it can be effectively argued that at a relatively early stage, it went for a strategic transformation by signifying its strategic thrust from memory chips to semiconductor devices. In this example, middle managers led the shift, which top management essentially ratified. The applications of strategic renewal have been found across different levels of analysis—including within and across firms, through various interfirm collaborative partnerships within industries and also across industries. This potential scope for strategic renewal suggests that it may have a wide and deep impact. Studies have been documented across many industries and over time depicting the displacement of existing market leaders by new entrants to an industry when technological change occurs. Other evidence, however, suggests that incumbent firms can withstand the onslaught of creative destruction through strategic renewal efforts that affect not only their own performance, but also the future of entire industries. It is a fact that established firms account for a significant share of growth of the industry. For example, a high chunk of share of new patents from innovation—often an important part of strategic renewal—comes from established firms and not from start-ups as could be expected. There are two enduring and time tested effects that are not fully recognized in studies that try to make a distinction between incumbent and new entrants in the industry. First, entrants that destroy the status quo in an industry are often established firms diversifying from other industries, rather than new entrants. Although start-ups make up the largest share of entrants into new markets, it is diversifying entrants that are the most successful in terms of both survival and performance in new industries. Diversifying entrants also play an important role in shaping the subsequent evolution and growth of new industries through investments they make in developing the necessary infrastructure and complementary assets.

As an illustration, L&T's and IBM's history of strategic renewal has been characterized by many important features of strategic renewal. It has included major transformations as well as incremental renewal. It has encompassed both strategic content and process, with both top and middle management playing important roles.

2.5 Avenues for strategic renewal

The above examples suggest that for any strategic renewal to happen, both content and process of change need to be understood. There are then important implications for companies, industries and also for entire economies. As mentioned earlier, strategic renewal has not received enough attention perhaps because of the complexity involved when compared to strategic change. As there are complexities involved in strategic renewal, many a time the concept of strategic renewal transcends beyond technological changes or the process part involved in the management of change. Thus the content and process parts of change are interlinked in the phenomenon of strategic renewal and could include multiple dimensions of change (see Tables 2.1 and 2.2).

Table 2.1 Four mechanisms for strategic renewal

Change methods Change Consequence	Spatial separation: Risk control is vital	Temporal separation: Speed is vital
Revitalizing some of the existing competencies	**Reanimating:** Bottom–up processes, typically double-loop leaning A middle–up process that may be especially suited to revitalizing existing competencies when speed is not vital but controlling risks is important	**Rejuvenating:** Holistic change programs aimed at revitalization A process that is most risky because the scope of the change is large and the content of the change is very difficult
Reordering core competencies and peripheral routines	**Venturing:** Top level processes of moving competencies around, including creating new units and selling old ones A process of change that is best suited to occasions where speed is not important and where the need to control risk is high	**Restructuring:** Top–down process of restructuring divisions, setting of new priorities and defining new products A process of change most suited to attempts to reorder processes when speed is important

Source: Adapted from Fuller and Volberda (1997)

Table 2.2 Technology and mechanisms of strategic renewal

	Competition is perceived benign by the firm; change is not urgent (Spatial)	Competition is perceived to be intense by the firm; change is urgent (Temporal)
Technologies new to the firm (revitalizing)	Slow change of core competence by local initiatives (peripheral change of core competence by animation)	Fast change of competencies by holistic, multilevel initiatives (fundamental change of core competence by rejuvenating)
Technologies existing in the firm (reordering)	Risk reduction by corporate venturing (technology variation by venturing)	Quick response by combining competencies across industries (managing technology convergence by restructuring)
Reordering core competencies and peripheral routines	**Venturing:** Top level processes of moving competencies around, including creating new units and selling old ones	**Restructuring:** Top–down process of restructuring divisions, setting of new priorities and defining new products
	A process of change that is best suited to occasions where speed is not important and where the need to control risk is high	A process of change most suited to attempts to reorder processes when speed is important

Source: Adapted from Fuller and Volberda (1997)

Seven steps that helped CEAT turn around

When Paras Chowdhary took over as the managing director of CEAT in 2001, he was thrilled to hear Chairman Harsh Goenka's assurance that he would get a free hand in running the company. But the caveat came swiftly: Chowdhary could ask for anything except money for additional investments.

It certainly wasn't music to his ears then, but the tyre industry veteran (Chowdhary was the CEO of Apollo Tyres for 11 out of the 22 years he spent there before joining the RPG Group) says he later understood Goenka's compulsions at that stage. CEAT was for all practical purposes a sick company in 2001. The Rs 14-crore (Rs 140 million) loss in that year was a lesser evil; what was particularly worrying was that the company was paying Rs 115 crore (Rs 1.15 billion) toward interest and depreciation. For a company with gross sales of just Rs 900 crore (Rs 9 billion), it was bad enough. Worse, both the loss as well as the interest amount were actually much more.

Here's why. CEAT then used to lend money to other group firms and charge interest on it which was considered as income. But the interest never came and the entire amount had to be ultimately written off.

Analysts estimated the actual loss in 2000–2001 at not less than Rs 60 crore (Rs 600 million) and the interest and depreciation at Rs 140 crore (Rs 1.4 billion). Chowdhary admits CEAT's identity was blurred at that stage—was it a tyre company or was it an investment company? "We were postponing our problems to the future. There were too many problems that were not immediately visible on the balance sheet," he says, sitting in his modest second-floor office at the RPG Group headquarters in Worli, Mumbai. So, in 2001, the problem looked quite complicated: CEAT was over-leveraged, it had no money to spend, no financial institution was willing to support it and raising money through the equity route was just not possible as the share price at that time was too low. There was more. No supplier was willing to give material unless the company cleared the dues of over Rs 150 crore (Rs 1.5 billion). And it was getting increasingly difficult to explain to the investing community and the board the reasons for the worsening profit margin vis-a-vis its competitors. Then there were legacy issues. Both its plants were in Maharashtra—one in Bhandup, a Mumbai suburb where the cost of operation was very high, and the other at Nashik. To ship its produce outside the state, the company had to pay huge octroi—a cost which its competitors who were well spread out weren't incurring. The factories were very old with practically no modernization efforts.

And since it was not a leader in the business, CEAT had to price its products 2 to 3 percent lower than its rivals. Analysts say CEAT's margins were hence around 5 percent lower than the competition. "In an industry where the profit margin has been traditionally low at 6 to 7 percent, you had it if your margin is 5 percent lower than competition," admits Chowdhary. The company's relatively small size only added to the problems.

Chowdhary had joined the RPG Group in 1997 but was heading the IT and telecom business for a peculiar reason: He had worked for Apollo long enough and didn't want to work for a rival tyre company. But in 2001, Goenka told him that CEAT "was in a difficult spot" and it would be great if he could take charge. Chowdhary knew that there were no easy answers to the problems that CEAT faced: He couldn't change the location of the factories, he didn't have the power to abolish octroi, he couldn't change the fact that Mumbai was a high cost city, he didn't have control over the fact that CEAT was an old company of 1960 vintage and hence carried a lot of baggage and, most important, he couldn't find any money to ride out of the crisis. Despite these handicaps, CEAT's transformation is an eye-opener. Consider the numbers first. The company's interest burden in 2008–2009 was Rs 91 crore (Rs 910 million)—less than 4 percent of its net sales of Rs 2,500 crore (Rs 25 billion).

In 2001, when he took charge, it was 13 percent of a relatively small base of net sales. Chowdhary is now aiming to bring that number down to 3 percent, despite higher capital expenditure. CEAT's operating profit before tax as a percentage of net sales has gone up to 13.5 percent in the first quarter of 2009–2010 from –1.7 percent in the previous year. Compare this with the corresponding figures of market leaders Apollo (12.1 percent from 6.9 percent) and JK (from 4 percent to 6.9 percent) and one starts getting a sense of the dramatic transformation.

Productivity in CEAT's two factories has gone up by nearly 50 percent since 2001 without much reduction in manpower. Chowdhary is candid enough to admit that all this has been possible partly due to luck but mostly because of some "real hard work" put in by his team members to implement a seven-fold turnaround strategy.

The turnaround

The first part of the strategy of course was to reduce the debt burden and thereby cut the interest payout. CEAT stopped all fresh investments as it was desperate to clean up its books. Result: CEAT has been repaying Rs 80 crore (Rs 800 million) debt every year. Its total debt, including working capital loans, is now just Rs 398 crore (Rs 3.98 billion).

Two, it decided to get into high-margin segments (90 percent of its products are now in that category) with a vengeance. That explains Chowdhary's drive to focus on the replacement market where the company's share in its total sales was just 50 percent. That figure went up to 75 percent in the first quarter of 2009–2010—something Chowdhary says was a dream fulfilled. The replacement market is important for tyre manufacturers as the consumers here don't mind paying extra for a quality product. But the fact is CEAT is the smallest player in radial tyres now with a monthly capacity of just 60,000 tyres against an average 200,000 of a couple of its competitors. To correct this, CEAT is setting up a grassroots radial plant at Halol in Gujarat at an investment of Rs 500 crore (Rs 5 billion) (half of that money will come from internal accruals). The plant, which will start production from August 2010 three months ahead of schedule, will have a monthly capacity to produce 180,000 tyres, taking its monthly production of radial tyres to 240,000.

Three, the company will start another plant at Ambarnath in Maharashtra by 2012, for which it has already been allotted 50 acres of land.

Four, it decided to get higher output from the two existing factories without making much investment. It was a difficult strategy to implement, but Chowdhary managed it by signing a long-term wage settlement with workers that was linked to productivity. A few anxious months later, the Bhandup plant production went up almost 50 percent. In the Nashik plant, production went up as much as 70 percent. "The extent of the productivity increase surprised me. Money is a great motivator and the capacity of human beings to deliver is infinite," Chowdhary says. The workers made sure that plants were open even on Sundays.

Five, the company put its might behind ensuring the quality of the products. Earlier, the quality of its products was acceptable, but not something that would create a customer pull. This was even more so as CEAT started targeting 20 percent of its revenues from the export market where profitability was good.

Six, Chowdhary made cost-cutting a religion for CEAT. So things such as better working capital management, manpower rationalization, reduction of administrative cost, cutting the commissions of the cost and forwarding agents became the new buzzwords. "For a Rs 2,500-crore company, we were even willing to question practices that could save us just Rs 25,000 annually," Chowdhary says. The cost of manpower will come down further once the Halol plant goes on stream because the salary of an industrial worker in Gujarat is at least 40 percent lower than his counterpart in Maharashtra where CEAT's two plants are now located.

And seven, Chowdhary's top team resorted to some smart buying of raw materials. For example, it imported 20,000 tonnes of natural rubber valued at Rs 200 crore (Rs 2 billion) in February/March 2009–2010 on a staggered shipment basis. That gave it a 20 percent cost advantage. Throughout the first and second quarter of the 2009/2010 financial year, CEAT consumed natural rubber that was bought at Rs 75–80 at a time when the ruling market price of the raw material has been hovering around Rs 90–108 for the last three–four months.

Eye on the future

Chowdhary says CEAT now wants to grow at 20 percent per annum against the industry average of 13–14 percent. And he is hopeful that the market share, which is at 14 percent now, will increase to 20 percent even on an expanded market in five to six years. If that happens, CEAT hopes to improve its position to become the third largest tyre company in India from fourth now. He also expects turnover to hit Rs 5,000 crore (Rs 50 billion) in FY 12 compared to an expected Rs 3,000 crore (Rs 30 billion) in the 2011–2012 financial year. That's easily achievable as the Gujarat plant alone is expected to contribute over Rs 1,000 crore (Rs 10 billion) in 2011–2012.

Competitors however are not losing any sleep. The chief executive of a rival tyre company says: "CEAT is doing better now, but that's just not enough." He adds the size of the company is too small compared to MRF, Apollo and even JK. Besides, CEAT, he says, has lacked a killer instinct and has been traditionally slow in responding to market requirements.

The problems of the past are also difficult to correct, he says. Chowdhary is aware of the problems, admitting: "It's true all the problems have not been corrected, but we have made good progress." That is reason enough for him to leave the office at 6 p.m. every day as he has put together a capable team that can steer the company even in his absence.

Goenka would nod in approval.

Source: www.rediff.com/money/slide-show/slide-show-1-7-steps-that-helped-ceat-turn-around/20091006.htm

References

Agarwal, R., & Helfat, C. E. (2009). Strategic renewal of organizations. *Organization Science, 20*(2), 281–293.
Fuller, C. B., & Volberda, H. W. (1997). Strategic renewal: How large complex organizations prepare for the future. *International Studies of Management & Organization, 27*(2), 95–120.

3   Building ambidexterity in organizations

3.1 Organizational ambidexterity

Organizational ambidexterity can be understood as an organization's ability to juggle between two contrasting work activities simultaneously. Simultaneous activities can be flexible manufacturing on one hand and manufacturing efficiency on the other, i.e. how the organization balances with both flexibility and efficiency. Similarly, organizations can work for differentiation and low cost strategic positioning and also the idea of global integration and local responsiveness. It was Tushman and O'Reilly (1996, 2004) who referred to ambidexterity as the ability of a firm to simultaneously demonstrate both continual (incremental) and discontinuous innovation and change. Thus the core issue in organizational ambidexterity is how organizations can create the needed balance between conflicting demands for exploitation and exploration.

3.2 Exploitation and exploration

There is a growing consensus around the view that exploration refers to learning and innovation and hence activities like search, variation, risk-taking, experimentation, play, flexibility, discovery and innovation are associated with exploration while exploitation refers to activities like refinement, choice, production, efficiency, selection, implementation and execution (March, 1991). Organizational adaptation requires both exploitation and exploration to achieve superior firm performance. Thus the simultaneous pursuit of both exploration and exploitation via loosely coupled and differentiated subunits or individuals, is an effective way for organizational adaptation. Exploitation refers to learnings through local search, through an experiential modification or reuse of current routines. Exploration in general refers to learnings achieved through processes of planned variation in experimentation.

Exploitative mechanisms are a general procedure of improvements in existing components and build on the existing technological path, whereas exploratory mechanisms involve a shift to a different technological path. Research studies have revealed that learning, improvement and acquisition of new knowledge are central to both exploitation and exploration.

Thus the terms "exploration" and "exploitation" have increasingly come to dominate organizational analyses of technological innovation, organization design, organizational adaptation, organizational learning, competitive advantage, organizational survival and growth. The essence of exploitation is the refinement and extension of existing competencies, technologies and paradigms. The essence of exploration is experimentation with new choices available. For example, R&D personnel can use "search and experiment" to find out newer mechanisms of producing a product/service, but the firm in which the R&D personnel work can attempt to exploit this newer mechanism for commercial purposes. It is also likely that routines which are of a repetitive nature may not involve much learning at the individual level (e.g. a shop floor operator repeatedly producing the same component daily). This does not mean there is no learning at the team or organizational level simply because of variability in skill levels, knowledge, experience and expertise across individuals. Thus at a team or departmental level, it is more likely that some learning from experience can be attributed because of the mentioned differences. This makes us realize that what one individual or team may view as search and experimental learning, another team or individual may view as exploitative or incremental learning.

However, exploitation and exploration as per theorists are mutually conflicting and are fundamentally incompatible because:

1. Exploration and exploitation compete for finite and scarce organizational resources. Thus, by definition, more resources devoted to exploitation would imply fewer resources left for exploration, and vice versa.
2. Both exploitative and explorative actions are self-reinforcing. It has been observed that because of higher variance of expected outputs in exploration, it has largely ended in failure. This failure in turn has a cascading effect for further newer ideas leading to more explorative actions leading to a failure trap. If we contrast this with efforts in exploitative actions—again purely by observation, we find initial encouraging results. The encouraging results have a positive reinforcement for further exploitative actions leading to a success

trap. Thus exploration often leads to more exploration, and exploitation to more exploitation.

3. The organizational systems and processes coupled with organizational culture and mindsets of managers needed for promoting exploration are radically different from those needed for promoting exploitation. Thus it is impossible to achieve simultaneous pursuit of the two. However, it is possible to question some of the key assumptions. Consider the arguments about the scarcity of resources. Although it is generally true that most organizational resources are finite, this need not be so for all types of resources. Some resources, such as information and knowledge, may be infinite. Also, organizations often have access not only to the resources that they own but also to resources in their external environments.

As an example let us look at Cisco. It is a firm operating in the high-technology domain. The nature of high technologies involved, coupled with the embedded designs make any product of Cisco to be of cutting edge. However, it also has a risk of high obsolescence. Thus it is imperative for the company to pursue a highly exploratory strategy with respect to technology and product development on a continual basis. Simultaneously, even the radically new and cutting-edge products can be manufactured, sold and serviced through a preexisting commercialization infrastructure that shows signs of evolving relatively slowly. In other words, the interfaces between product R&D on the one hand and manufacturing, sales and service on the other are relatively standardized. However, the resources needed for product development and R&D are fundamentally different from those needed for complementary downstream activities. As such, it is easy to imagine that Cisco could simultaneously engage in a high degree of exploration in product R&D and a high rate of exploitation in complementary downstream domains such as manufacturing, sales and service. Examination of recent studies has revealed that firms operate in multiple domains, not all of which are tightly coupled via specialized interfaces.

Thus the scarcer the resources needed to pursue both exploration and exploitation, the greater the likelihood that the two will be mutually exclusive—that is, high values of one will necessarily imply low values of the other.

3.3 Types of ambidexterity

Developments in the field of ambidexterity have identified at least three forms through which firms attain a balance between exploration and exploitation:

a) *Structural*: In structural ambidexterity companies maintain organizational separation of their traditional businesses and their new exploratory ventures through loosely coupled dual structures. This separation could be exhibited if one looks at the structure, processes, systems and culture in both the traditional and new ventures. But the separation at the levels mentioned is backed by a strong link at the senior level across all units of the organization.

b) *Temporal/punctuated equilibrium*: Punctuated equilibrium refers to temporal rather than organizational differentiation and suggests that cycling through periods of exploration and exploitation is a more viable approach than a simultaneous pursuit of the two. As may be clear, ambidexterity and punctuated equilibrium are radically different mechanisms.

c) *Contextual ambidexterity*: This construct of ambidexterity through the contextual route is defined as a capability that arises out of the behavioral pattern of a performance center (business unit) to juggle between the need to align and adapt simultaneously. Alignment can be defined in terms of how multiple business units in organizations work together to display a synergistic effect and cohesion in their working styles ultimately leading to achievement of the wider organizational goals. Similarly, adaptability can be understood to be the ability of a business unit to quickly adjust and refocus on activities in order to prescribe to the ever-changing demands in the task environment.

Initial emphasis in the field of ambidexterity was centered on structural and temporal design solutions that enabled organizations to overcome the competing demands of exploration and exploitation. More recent research, however, uncovered other solutions that could promote ambidexterity. Organizational contexts of performance management and social aspects like support and trust are also capable of fostering ambidexterity in organizations. Moreover, contextual ambidexterity lets the decisions of ambidexterity be made at the individual/team level. Unlike structural ambidexterity which can be built by developing "dual structural mechanisms," contextual ambidexterity is best realized in a business unit by developing systems, processes, values, beliefs and norms that empower employees in organizations. This empowerment through context can be understood in terms of how an individual devotes time shuffling between the need to align as well as adapt.

Alignment activities are geared toward improving firm performance in the short term and adaptability activities are geared for creating for the long term. Several studies have reported that business units where characteristics of exploration were encouraged and exploitation was not given adequate importance have suffered huge costs of experimentation without gaining significant benefits. Conversely studies have also been made in which systems in a business unit that encourage exploitation but exclude exploration are also not likely to get optimal benefits. For survival and prosperity, a business unit needs to develop the twin abilities at the same time. A large majority of studies in the field have employed a firm/business unit level of analysis with relatively few attempts at addressing multilevels of analysis in the same study. Ambidexterity questions in firms have been argued to be "nested" in nature. Ambidexterity transpires at multiple levels in the organization simultaneously.

One work in the field of ambidexterity deserves special mention in this book. Adler, Goldoftas and Levine (1999), in their seminal study, discuss the Toyota Production System as applied to the NUMMI plant (co-owned by GM and Toyota). Reconciling the "paradox" of flexibility and efficiency, the authors suggest four mechanisms that help shift the trade-offs between the two goals: metaroutines; job enrichment; switching; and partitioning.

Metaroutines. The concept of routines is not new to the field of strategic management and organizational studies. Organizational routines are defined as a general term for all regular and predictable behavioral patterns of firms. Organizational routines literature suggests three kinds of routines: metaroutines (higher order routines bringing about changes in lower level organizational routines); decision-making routines (routines aiding in strategic decisions like investment, pricing, etc.); and operating routines (standardized procedures for day to day activities).

Job enrichment. Job enrichment is about creating a context in the organization whereby individuals and teams take responsibility in dividing their time in terms of how much time to spend on exploration and how much on exploitative activities thereby enriching their work profiles.

Switching. Switching is a mechanism by which organizations shift between periods of exploration followed by periods of exploitation across time horizons. In switching organizations shift between periodic bursts of alignment and adaptability.

Partitioning. Partitioning entails the creation of separate organizational units: a typically small, decentralized exploratory unit with loose processes separated from a larger exploitation unit with tight processes. Spatial separation focused on standalone units with different brand name, structures, culture and processes. Pure spatial separation, although, helps organizations to separate the tensions inherent within exploration and exploitation but does not allow for the possibility of utilizing synergies between the two separated units.

It can be effectively argued that job enrichment, switching and partitioning have significant overlaps with contextual, temporal and structural ambidexterity respectively. Metaroutines shift the trade-off between efficiency and flexibility by transforming non-routine tasks into routine ones using either "advanced automation" or "organizational means." However, meta- or high level routines have not been studied significantly in ambidexterity literature. It is also unclear whether metaroutines are indeed a distinct mechanism or if they coalesce with the established trio of ambidexterity types.

3.4 Ambidextrous managers and organizations: the challenge

The senior level team in organizations should be adept at developing skills of mental balancing in terms of not only gazing forward in the horizon to prepare for breakthrough innovations that will define the future but also constantly look backward attending to the products of the past. Studies of organizations have revealed that many successful and reputed organizations are way ahead of the competition in continuously renewing their present market offerings; however, when it comes to offering breakthrough new products and services, these organizations stumble and fall. The failure to achieve breakthrough innovations while also making steady improvements to an existing business is so common yet so fascinating that it has become the management hot spot in terms of understanding what companies should do and what they should not do. As such what should an organization do to solve this unique challenge? What are the challenges that face established organizations in achieving breakthroughs when they attempt to pursue innovations that lie beyond their current products or markets? Do they succeed in achieving breakthroughs? Does their existing business suffer? What organizational and managerial structures do they use? What works and what does not? Research done by Tushman and O'Reilly (1996, 2004) found that companies that have actually been quite successful at both exploiting the present and exploring the future share important characteristics. These companies have found a way to maintain organization separation of their traditional businesses and their new exploratory ventures. This separation could be exhibited if one looks at the structure, processes, systems and culture in both the traditional and new ventures. But the separation at the levels mentioned is backed by a strong link at the senior level across all units of the organization. Thus the organization manages to balance the tension of separation across units but also maintains tight integration at the senior executive level.

If we study the kinds of innovation pursued in companies, they can broadly be classified into two types: (i) incremental innovations; and (ii) radical breakthrough innovations. The performance of the organizations focused on small incremental innovations in traditional organizations vis-a-vis radical innovations have a direct impact on a firm's strategy and culture, and design of the processes and systems. The characteristics of ambidexterity allow organizations to outperform traditional organizations, because of its inherent capabilities of cross-fertilization of ideas; on deeper analysis the management model would reveal the sync in senior managerial coordination across each of the loose units. The sheer structure of an ambidextrous organization ensures integration on allocation of resources, talent, expertise, customers, etc. on the lines of a typical traditional organization, but simultaneously the organizational separation allows for the new unit's unique strategies, structures, processes and culture to be nurtured separately and remain insulated from the culture of the traditional organization. This explains why in any traditional organization, the established units can focus their energies in constantly refining their own products and not get overwhelmed by the responsibility for path-breaking innovations, which should be left to the new unit to explore.

If we observe that there is a pattern across industries in which success often precedes failure studies are not very helpful for illustrating what actually went wrong during the failure period, as the organization must have been doing similar things in the past. It is just that what brought them past success was not an enabler for future success. Thus it is imperative for the managements of many organizations to understand the timing of innovation and change. The real challenge of leadership is to find ways and means to be able to compete successfully by both increasing the fit among strategy, structure, culture and processes, while simultaneously preparing the organization for the inevitable disruptions required by discontinuous environmental change. The key word stressed here is "simultaneously." Unfortunately, focusing on either of the skill sets guarantees short-term success but long-term failure. This precisely explains why managers need to do both at the same time, that is, they need to be ambidextrous. The metaphor of ambidexterity is exemplified by a juggler in a circus. A juggler who can be very good at keeping up a single ball is not interesting and it does not test his or her skills. A juggler who can handle multiple balls at the same time makes an interesting show.

3.5 Patterns of organization evolution

Patterns on how organizations evolve are not unique. Many successful organizations juggle between periods of incremental and transformational changes for most of their history. These discontinuities or disruptions may be driven by technology, competitors, regulatory events or significant changes in economic and political conditions and could involve either proactive or reactive changes. For example, deregulation and changes in government policies in the telecom and airline industries in India led to waves of mergers and failures as firms scrambled to reorient themselves to the new competitive environment. These changes in the environment have shifted the basis on which firms compete in these markets. If we observe the computer industry, technological changes in microprocessor technology have caused huge disruptions and altered the face of the industry. As such firms which had believed in congruence for larger parts of their history and organization success soon faced huge challenges with the discontinuities. It is imperative that today's organizations should no longer feel that their competitive landscape is going to be stable. This is an increasingly unlikely condition in today's world and firms must be prepared to confront revolutionary changes.

Managers in organizations for the short term should definitely go for the alignment of the people processes with the structure to match the strategies so that the evolutionary changes in the industry could be understood better. But this by itself is not sufficient for sustained success. In the long run, managers may be required to destroy or disrupt the fit that has made their organizations successful. The immediate translation of these phenomena for managers would mean continuously shifting between periods characterized by relative stability and incremental innovation, and part of the time grappling with revolutionary changes. These contradicting managerial expectations require that managers periodically need to renew themselves by shedding their old ways of working so that a new organization can be rebuilt or recreated that can tackle the environmental complexities much better and much faster. This explains why managers need to be ambidextrous and firms by virtue of their ambidextrous characteristic separate the great from the good organizations.

Thus thriving with contradictory characteristics within the organization is needed for the build up to an ambidextrous organization. There are good illustrations of firms and managers who have succeeded in balancing these tensions. To drive the point of ambidexterity in terms of how organizations handle it in practicality, illustrations are drawn from three different industries, Hewlett Packard (IT/technology), Johnson and Johnson (J&J) (consumer products/pharmaceuticals) and ABB (electrical goods industry). Each of these has been able to compete in mature market segments through incremental changes and in emerging markets and technologies through disruptive innovation. Each of the firms has been successful at winning by engaging both aspects of exploitation and exploration.

At one level these are firms pursuing similar revolutions. HP competes in markets like instruments, computers and networks; J&J in consumer products, pharmaceuticals and professional medical products. Similarly, ABB competes in areas like designing to execution of power plants, electrical equipment, transportation systems and environmental controls. But the significance of each of these companies in the context of ambidexterity is that each of them has revitalized itself periodically both with incremental and radical innovations. HP has evolved from an instrument manufacturer to a computer manufacturer and now to a company which offers network-based solutions. J&J has moved from consumer products to pharmaceuticals. The transformation in ABB has been brought about with the merger of Asea and Brown Boveri, wherein from a slow heavy engineering company the company is now a big time player in the electrical and control systems across major parts of the globe.

Organizational architectures

Although the combined employee strength of these three companies represents over 3 lakhs (300,000), each has found a common way to remain small and agile by emphasizing autonomous groups. For instance, J&J has over 150 separate operating companies that constantly scan the environment for new market opportunities. ABB on the other hand has over 5,000 profit centers with the average size of a profit center capped at 50 people. These centers operate like independent small businesses each having the responsibility of a profit center. HP has over 50 separate divisions in its fold and the headquarters splits the divisions whenever a unit gets larger than a thousand or so people. The reasoning given is to keep units small and autonomous, so that employees feel a sense of ownership and are responsible for their own results, and above all make the organization agile and nimble footed. This encourages a culture of autonomy and risk-taking which is conspicuous in its absence in large centralized organizations.

However, this does mean that the nimble footedness of each of these players comes at the cost of reducing the overall size of the companies in terms of scale and scope. All three companies manage to retain the benefits of size, especially in marketing and manufacturing. If we observe carefully ABB continuously scans and reevaluates where to set up its worldwide manufacturing sites. Similarly, J&J uses its brand power and marketing insights to leverage new products and technologies which can be used for new markets or to find new applications. Similarly, the market power and reach are utilized by HP which leverages the relationship built with retailers of its printer business to market and distribute its new personal computers line. In each of these firms, size is used to leverage economies of scale and scope, not to ensure administrative control that can slow the organization down. The emphasis is on customer centricity—decisions taken as close to the customer as possible. Reward systems are designed to be appropriate to the nature of the business unit and emphasize results based on intrapreneurial abilities and risk-taking. Percy Barnevik, the legendary CEO of ABB characterizes this as his 7–3 formula. The emphasis is always on taking decisions—he goes on to say that it is always better to be decisive—rather than wasting time to find the right solution it is always beneficial to take decisions and be right in seven out of ten points. At J&J managers at senior levels have high capacities to bear with well-intentioned failures. Thus a fine balance is struck between size and speed, centralization and autonomy. Even while autonomy and decentralization is practiced, each of these companies ensures that individual and team accountabilities are monitored with proper control systems in place.

Multiple cultures within the same organization

A common overarching culture is the glue that binds these companies together. The key aspect in each of these firms is the importance placed on a strong, widely shared corporate culture to promote company-wide integration and to encourage identification and sharing of information and resources, which is bound to be pulled in different directions unless there are shared values to be adhered to. The culture in each of the organizations promotes and nurtures trust, stretch, discipline and support. Take any of the code of conduct norms—Credo at J&J, the HP way or ABB's policy bible—these norms and values provide the glue that keeps these organizations together. The paradox of these conduct norms is that the same company also has varying sub-cultures for some of its business units.

Thus the management model in each of the organizations promotes both tightness and loosely defined cultures simultaneously which is a mandatory aspect of building ambidexterity. The overarching sense of purpose is supported by supportive leaders who both encourage the culture and know enough to allow appropriate variations to occur across various units. If we see how the very successful printer business evolved at HP, it was all because of the entrepreneurial flair of a small group of managers who had the freedom to pursue the idea, rather than any strategic foresight of top management. Similar approaches are used at J&J and ABB to enter new markets or develop new technologies without burdened bureaucratic control systems hanging over them. On the other hand, in return for the autonomy granted, employees have to deliver results and effective performance standards are drawn up. Managing units that pursue widely different strategies and that have varied structures and cultures is a classic act of jugglery which many a manager is not comfortable with confronting. This is described in ABB as preaching and persuading.

Great organizations handle this tension through the relatively long tenure some managers have in these organizations and the continual reinforcement of the embedded supporting systems. Often leaders in these organizations embody the overarching culture and act as visible representers of it.

It is a paradox that ambidextrous organizations learn by the same instincts that sometimes kill successful firms in terms of variation, selection and retention. They promote variation through strong efforts to decentralize, to eliminate bureaucracy, to encourage individual autonomy and accountability, and experiment and take risks so that the organization remains nimble footed. Managers must be ready to cannibalize their own business at times of industry transitions. While this may sound theatrical, these organizational transitions are quite difficult in practice. Success brings with it inertia and dynamic conservatism leading to complacency and arrogance even to the best of organizations. While there are clear benefits to proactive change, only a miniscule number of farsighted firms initiate discontinuous change before a performance decline. At Intel the legendary Andy Grove made a remark once which has become prophetic, "There is at least one point in the history of any company when you have to change dramatically to rise to the next performance level. Miss the moment and you start to decline."

3.6 The scope of the ambidextrous organization

The profoundness of business scope that ambidextrous organizations encounter can be summed up in two distinct ways—ambidextrous organizations focus both on exploiting existing capabilities and exploring new opportunities at the same time. Table 3.1 elucidates the critical alignments between exploitation and exploration.

Ambidextrous leadership. Different alignments held cohesively through senior team integration, common shared values and common senior team rewards. The senior level team in organizations should be committed to encourage and promote ambidexterity; resistance at the top levels of an organization cannot be tolerated, which means that a shift to an ambidextrous organization can be a nerve wrenching experience.

The aspirations provided by a clear and distinct vision of top management to promote ambidexterity wherein the overarching goal that permits exploitation and exploration to coexist should stringently permeate organizations because of strong organizational inertia that exists in every organization. The senior level team in organizations should always be looked upon as enablers of change. The legacies of once successful firms that have fallen on hard times or gone out of business underscore the fact that success makes organizations arrogant and complacency sets in, and that is precisely the starting point of decline in organizations.

Established companies in matured businesses can revitalize themselves through the periodic shift between incremental and breakthrough products and processes, and it is this ability to build new businesses

Table 3.1 Alignments of exploitation and exploration

Alignment	Exploitative	Exploratory
Strategic intent	Cost, profit	Innovations, growth
Critical tasks	Operations, efficiency, incremental innovation	Adaptability, new products, breakthrough innovation
Competencies	Operational	Entrepreneurial
Structure	Formal, mechanistic	Adaptive, loose
Controls, rewards	Margins, productivity	Milestones, growth
Culture	Efficiency, low risk, quality, customers	Risk-taking, speed, flexibility, experimentation
Leadership role	Authoritative, top–down	Visionary, involved

Source: O'Reilly and Tushman (2004)

without destroying its traditional businesses, that is the hall mark of an ambidextrous company. Thus the top managers in ambidextrous organizations should be adept at structuring the organization to combine organizational separation at the business level and at the same time integrate at the corporate level.

The above discussion makes us ponder the possible links between environmental dynamism and ambidexterity developed in organizations. As has been already mentioned, there is a possibility that high levels of ambidextrous characteristics exhibited by organizations are a fallout of higher environmental dynamism. Though organizational ambidexterity is a new research paradigm in organization theory, several issues fundamental to this broad construct remain controversial. Some of the critical tensions that are debatable are as follows:

a) Should ambidexterity be pursued in organizations through differentiation or through an integration route?
b) Is identification of ambidexterity a characteristic occurrence at the individual or organizational level?
c) Should organizations take a static or dynamic perspective on ambidexterity?
d) Does ambidexterity arise internally from within the firm, or is it a process of externalizing some processes?

Researchers have recognized the roles of differentiation and integration as mechanisms for enabling organizations to deliver effectively. However, the majority of the ambidexterity researchers have focused either on differentiation or on integration. This structural differentiation helps ambidextrous organizations maintain different competencies with which to address inconsistent demands arising from emerging and mainstream business opportunities. The other view has focused on integration, that is, the behavioral capacity mechanisms that enable organizations to address exploitation and exploration activities within the same unit. The need to combine processes for differentiation and integration creates a paradox that is difficult to resolve. To manage paradox, it is not a case of either–or trade-off but how one can capture the extremes creatively. The arguments presented above can be summarized in three observations that should be explored further. First, integration and differentiation are complementary, not alternative, mechanisms for achieving organizational effectiveness. Second, the relative balance between integration and differentiation will vary depending upon the task undertaken. The third issue as a result of the other two indicates that continued and committed managerial attention is needed to manage the trade-offs between integration and differentiation. Consequently, a business unit may become ambidextrous by creating two functions or subdivisions with different foci. A manufacturing plant may become ambidextrous by creating two sets of different teams, one team in charge of exploration and the other team in charge of exploitation and a single team may become ambidextrous by allocating different roles to each individual.

Several studies on contextual ambidexterity focus on the cultural aspects of the contextual behavior compared to structural characteristics. Teams that focus on creativity and exploration differ in their personality traits, from teams that emphasize exploitation activities. Although these studies observe that some managers seem to be able to take on contradictory tasks, they fail to explain why these managers—as opposed to others—are able to do so. Answering this question may require exploring managers' personal characteristics. For example, the ability to engage in paradoxical thinking may be vital for effectively managing exploitation and exploration. Thus individuals possessing relevant knowledge of the issue at hand need to combine linkages between past and new knowledge.

Besides personal characteristics, factors related to the organization also aid in making employees act ambidextrously. Socialization mechanisms in organizations, how recognition is given to employees and team-building practices aid in helping employees in organizations act ambidextrously. Development of appropriate organizational contexts also helps managers in shuffling between alignment and adaptability oriented activities. Similarly behavioral integration—the senior team's wholeness and unity of effort—can help process disparate demands. Formal senior team contingency rewards and informal senior team social integration are also important mechanisms to enable senior teams to host contradictory forces. All these studies provide a strong indication that organizational factors have to be considered alongside personal characteristics when explaining individuals' ambidexterity. Further, personal and organizational factors may be closely interrelated. Thus ambidexterity is a function of both organizational and individual effects which are closely related.

Managing organizations for the simultaneous pursuit of exploitation and exploration may thus be a task of dynamic rather than static alignment. If we look through the lens of structural ambidexterity, how an organization comprising structurally differentiated units evolves over time is not clear. Companies have demonstrated structurally differentiated units that remain highly autonomous over time, for example the premium coffee maker Nespresso remained a fully autonomous unit within the food industry leader Nestlé Group for more than two decades. It is also pointed out in a case study that though the autonomous nature of Xerox's Palo Alto Research Center (PARC) existed for decades, the level of cross-unit integration increased among the research center and other units as time progressed. Though the established fact is that human brains are designed to be ambidextrous, it is common wisdom that sequential ambidexterity is easier to achieve at the individual level than simultaneous ambidexterity.

The specific arguments made above can be summarized in the form of the following generalizations: (a) managing ambidexterity requires a dynamic alignment of the tasks at hand; (b) sustainability of ambidexterity in organizations requires both the structural and contextual route over time; (c) ambidexterity may arise from both simultaneous and sequential attention to exploitation and exploration periodically. Ambidexterity may imply the managerial challenge of not only balancing exploitation and exploration but also of integrating external and internal knowledge. Top management can use economic, structural, social and cognitive influences to enable middle managers to carry out these linking activities.

The findings show that ambidexterity is fostered by close interrelations between existing and new knowledge. A synergistic effect can be achieved by allowing existing resources to be more fully employed to acquire new capabilities and also by permitting new knowledge to be more fully integrated into the existing pool of resources. Thus differentiation approaches need to be combined with integrative efforts to arrive at peak ambidexterity characteristics.

Appendix

Effects of metaroutines on multilevel ambidexterity: The case of new product introduction at Tata Motors, India

The study focuses on the role of metaroutines in shaping the form of the ambidexterity question. A continuum between paradoxes (lower number of constraints) and trade-offs (higher number of constraints) is visualized. At the strategic level, without taking detailed functional constraints into account, firms can consider ambidexterity as a paradoxical question. This approach helps in justifying the idea that exploration and exploitation are necessary, though conflicting, objectives of a firm (March, 1991). A firm would like to maximize its performance in both fields. However, at the operational level, while considering detailed constraints and boundaries, the same ambidexterity question could convert into a trade-off as the original unbounded paradox gets bound by multiple layers of constraints.

Findings

New product development in an automotive firm is a highly complex process with the presence of many nested ambidexterity questions. At a product level, each product can be visualized as an exploration to best suit the identified customer segment with a brand new assembly of a host of components. However, at the functional level, each product is a mixture of exploration and exploitation of capabilities, competencies and resources. For example, the sourcing function within the firm has to balance exploration and exploitation of components within a given new product design. New components help in addressing unique needs of the targeted customer segment and identified technology, while the use of existing components helps the firm significantly in reducing the overall cost of product development and manufacturing. Similarly, each functional element within Tata Motors faces the tension between exploration and exploitation nested within the overall exploration of a new product.

In 2001, Tata Motors recorded the worst loss (Rs 500 crore (Rs 5 billion)) in the history of the Indian private sector. The loss was in large part due to the significant sensitivity of the firm's product portfolio to cyclical economic downturns. The jolt from the firm's financial performance led to a new strategic plan focusing on three aspects: "cost reduction, quality improvement and new product introduction" (Palepu & Srinivasan, 2004, p. 7). Following the strategic plan and the vision of its leaders, Tata Motors in subsequent years launched some innovative and path-breaking vehicles like the Ace (commercial) and Nano (passenger) among others. Tata Motors' product portfolio consists broadly of two divisions focused on the commercial and passenger vehicles respectively. Since 2001, the common theme of many launches was the use of the new product introduction (NPI) metaroutine. A launch might refer to the introduction of a brand new platform or cosmetic changes to an existing vehicle. Hence, a given launch might vary significantly from another on the basis of the exploration required for each.

In Tata Motors, NPI is a metaroutine because it refers to a pattern of actions spanning processes, structure and governance that lead to the creation of product level operating routines in manufacturing, sourcing and marketing. The schematic details of the metaroutine are presented below.

The new product introduction metaroutine process

The NPI metaroutine includes a standardized and documented process initially created with aid from the Warwick Manufacturing

Group, U.K. One of the first vehicles to utilize the complete NPI process in Tata Motors between 2001 and 2005 was Tata Ace. Since then, multiple product launches have seen the maturation and evolution of the process within the firm. Currently, the metaroutine is in its third generation of maturity encompassing all NPI projects in Tata Motors, but retains the core elements introduced during the development of Tata Ace. The metaroutine is a multi-stage tailored process starting at the identification of customer segment opportunities identified at the strategic level and ending shortly after the launch of the vehicle.

A manager who worked on the initial implementations of the metaroutine for Tata Ace stated:

> Before Ace, for ex Indica and Indigo (previous product launches), the ERC (R&D group) used to be in charge of the new product development process…new products were generally reactions to competitor developments or worldwide automobile trends.

Based on the inputs from the Strategic Business Planning Group (a strategic group), the Portfolio Planning Group (a Business Unit Level group) manages a Product Portfolio Plan for the Business Unit. Individual product recommendations within the Product Portfolio Plan are then approved at a strategic level based on the inputs from various marketing, engineering and sourcing trends. The approval of an individual vehicle development kicks off an iteration of the NPI metaroutine.

The concept development stage

The metaroutine begins with the concept development stage. In this stage, the targeted customer segment and the potential market are finalized. Further, the broad guidelines on the product concept are finalized after exploring existing market offerings using benchmarking, assessing the feasibility and benefits of the identified concept. A comprehensive "voice of the customer" analysis is also done facilitated by senior marketing personnel, for completely new vehicle launches. A senior management member in charge of portions of the NPI process noted:

> Before going to market and doing a market research, the firm created a target framework. The organization said that we need to earn so much and invest only this much at the maximum.

Given the target framework, the NPI process demands an exhaustive "voice of customer" (VOC) analysis done using a detailed and pre-designed questionnaire. The VOC analysis converts customer feedback to technical specifications detailed to the aggregate component level of the vehicle (e.g. engine, interiors, etc.). The identified concept is also detailed with a boundary specification, features, scope, quality, scale and business case freeze.

Engineering development

The next phase in the metaroutine is the engineering development phase which encompasses three stages. This stage receives the deliverables of the previous stage and builds on them. This phase initially focuses on the balancing and refining of the product design. After the design is detailed and finalized, the product is engineered and validated using virtual and physical testing. In this stage, the focus is on product engineering and hence the R&D function dominates the actions taken. However, parallel production process engineers and sourcing department are also involved using processes like 3P. In the lean manufacturing world "3P" (Production, Preparation, Process) is a method for product and production design. The goal is to develop a process or product that meets customer requirements in the "least-waste way." Their role is to understand and plan for the manufacturing requirements based on the changes and refinements in design.

The validation and production testing

This phase follows the engineering development phase. It involves the testing of the production facility and process proving. By this phase, the design has been completely frozen and the production routines are finalized after rigorous validation.

Start of sales and a final review

The final phase of the NPI process deals with the start of sales and a final review of the product performance and functional routines. After this stage, operating routines of production, sourcing and marketing are transferred to existing groups within each functional department and only minor modifications to the product design and routines are allowed, primarily to deal with warranty issues and possible field failures. Such changes are handled outside the NPI metaroutine and the resulting changes in design/manufacturing are updated in a centrally maintained information system.

Structure

All phases discussed above are tied to pre-specified structural groups and profiles. In parallel to the launch of the NPI metaroutine, Tata Motors, in 2003, had introduced the matrix structure focusing on direct and indirect reporting of individuals. While personnel directly report to their functional supervisors, they also report indirectly to product planning and vehicle level teams.

Each NPI project is handled by a separate, centralized planning and project management group within Tata Motors. The NPI metaroutine is owned by the group which has multiple roles. In the concept development phase, each project is handled by a pre-defined team structure, headed by a team lead from the centralized planning and project management group, with senior cross-functional members from Marketing, Design, Sourcing, Business Planning, etc.

Before the beginning of the engineering development phase, the project responsibility is handed over to a Vehicle Line Director. The Director is responsible for the setting and execution of the vehicle level team which comprises of members from almost all major functions in the firm. Further, the present NPI process also mandates functional team leaders who act as a Project Manager within their function. Midway through the engineering concept phase, a Launch Manager is allocated to the project. The Launch Manager, a member of the planning and project management group, reports to the corresponding Plant Head and is responsible for the remaining stages of the NPI metaroutine. The NPI metaroutine structure has evolved over the years from a light-weight organization to a heavier version with further refinement and accountability of roles.

Tailoring

The NPI metaroutine, at Tata Motors, has matured considerably over the past decade. During this maturation, the metaroutine has added significant, in-built, mechanisms to promote tailoring of the process and structures based on the scale and scope of the project. The calculation of the project scale is based on the degree of change envisioned in key vehicle level attributes like body changes, electricals and manufacturing location. The decision on the scale categorization has wide-ranging predetermined effects on the vehicle level team size, project duration and the degree of involvement of team members. Additionally, the requirement and complexity of artifacts are also reduced for lower scale projects.

The scope of the project delves into the choices of carryover/modification/newness of the vehicle attributes and components. A carryover strategy is formulated during the concept definition stage. Another key mechanism promoted by the firm, in its NPI metaroutine, is the practice of specifying a commonality index which each vehicle level team adheres to. The commonality index sets the ratio of components of a new vehicle that will be shared with other existing vehicle platforms in Tata Motors. After the concept development phase and first portion of the engineering development phase, the commonality index becomes fixed for the remaining stages of the NPI metaroutine. Commonality of components has many benefits for Tata Motors. First, the costs of shared components are lower as with large volumes the firms can generally negotiate lower rates from the component suppliers. Further, the features and performance of pre-used components are known and controllable by the firm as compared to exploratory one-off component designs for new vehicles. Also, the total time and effort of the new product development team can be focused on a defined set of new components rather than attempting to re-analyze the fit and efficiency of each component in a vehicle.

NPI at Tata Motors is a mix of exploration and exploitation questions across levels of analysis. At the strategic level, each new vehicle is an innovation for the firm and the market. However, at the functional level, each vehicle becomes a mix of exploration and exploitation as an individual product might exploit previously used sub-assemblies, marketing strategy, vendors, etc. Managing and shaping these different questions across different levels defines the firm's ambidexterity.

The role of the NPI metaroutine in Tata Motors, India raises some interesting theoretical questions pertaining to ambidexterity. Although, the NPI metaroutine decides on the new product details as well as the manufacturing, sourcing and marketing strategies, the metaroutine's life is only until the launch and ramp-up of the new product and its associated business model. After the ramp-up of production, the implementation responsibility of the decisions made by the NPI metaroutine are transferred to the existing domains (manufacturing, sourcing, marketing, etc.) and the NPI metaroutine ceases. Although, annual review processes of launched vehicles are undertaken by the vehicle level organization structure, any major changes in the vehicle need the invocation of a new NPI metaroutine iteration. Also, although the NPI metaroutine is centralized as a function of Tata Motors, each instance of the metaroutine involves a group of employees who are partitioned until the completion of the metaroutine.

The NPI metaroutine at Tata Motors includes the process, structural, timing and contextual aspects of ambidexterity (Adler et al., 1999). The NPI process is mapped in detail to the structure of the strategic, vehicle level teams and functional team leads. The key responsibilities of each member participating in the metaroutine are pre-decided and fixed. Although, iterations of the metaroutine may involve different actors, the structural role, context and duration of each actor's involvement are pre-defined based on scale and scope categorization majorly done during the concept development stage.

Further, through extensive target setting, the strategic team involved in the metaroutine reduces the set of acceptable solutions for each functional group. For example, the freeze of a commonality index, mandating a fixed ratio of parts that need to be exploited in the development of a new vehicle, reduces the set of possible solutions for the product design and sourcing functions. In case the groups are not able to attain the overall commonality index for a vehicle, a pre-defined exception handling process is invoked which requires signoffs at various strategic levels. Hence, in a given sub-iteration of the metaroutine, the functional groups work on the new vehicle by freezing the commonality index. This suggests that the metaroutine not only affects the exploration of processes and structures, but, also affects the exploration of functional content used in a new vehicle.

Finally, the NPI metaroutine mandates the creation of detailed artifacts and status reports. Hence, problem solving techniques and the final solutions arrived at in previous vehicle launches are available to all future NPI metaroutine iterations. By referencing previous NPI artifacts, a team can reduce the exploration required to solve a particular problem faced while introducing a new product.

a) Reshaping paradoxical ambidexterity to trade-off questions at vehicle and functional levels—the ambidexterity questions at different levels in Tata Motors are a mixture of paradoxes and trade-offs. At the strategic and business unit level, after the loss incurred in 2001, the firm wanted to exploit its existing products and explore new customer segments. At the product level, also, the strategic and NPI core team attempt to combine the customer centric explorations with exploitations resulting in cost savings. The ambidexterity questions at these two levels appear to be paradoxes for strategic team members. However, in the case of functional domains, each individual domain was working under increased constraints due to the NPI metaroutine. Hence, the ambidexterity questions at the domain/functional level seem to be a trade-off based on the constraints of cost, quality and features faced by individual functional domains. An example of the transition from paradoxes to trade-offs is presented for Tata Ace Engine selection. These findings are visualized in Figure 3A.2.

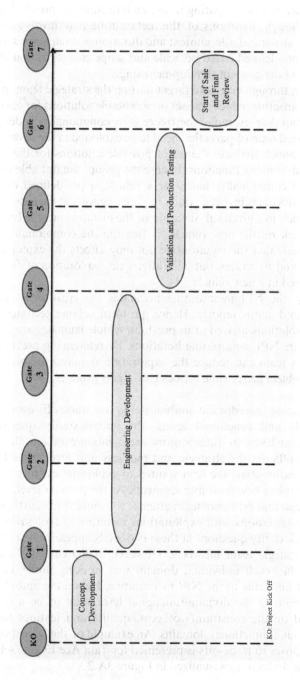

Figure 3A.1 Illustrative generalized depiction of NPI stages

Source: Interviews and Palepu and Srinivasan (2004)

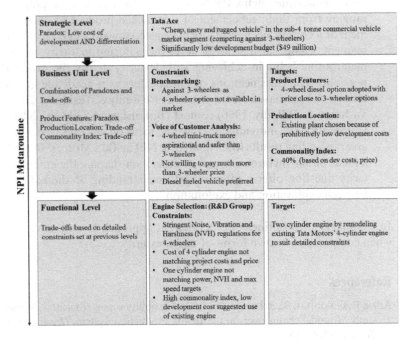

Figure 3A.2 Examples of constraint/target setting across levels: Tata Ace engine selection

Excerpts from the presentation made by Saurav Snehvrat and Swarup Kumar Dutta at Special Conference of Strategic Management Society, Hong Kong, December 2016.

Source: Interviews and Palepu and Srinivasan (2004)

b) Effectively, as the NPI metaroutine progresses from the strategic to a functional level, the introduction and freezing of various constraints on cost, quality, commonality, duration, etc. convert a paradoxical ambidexterity question to a manageable trade-off at each functional level. Hence, the metaroutine not only reduces the total exploration required for a new vehicle, but, also changes the nature of ambidexterity questions posed to functional levels.

c) Tailoring: The scale of an iteration of the NPI metaroutine is calculated using a set process, structure and mechanism, as described above. The setting of the scale of the new product implicitly sets the overall exploration expected out of the metaroutine iteration. Further, based on the scale calculations the number and type of resources, their level of involvement, the overall process and structural requirements are tailored. This tailoring, in-built in the

NPI metaroutine, helps the firm to address a variety of projects ranging from slight refinement of a launched product to development of a completely new platform targeted toward a new customer segment. Hence, at a strategic level the tailoring maturity of the metaroutine helps in achieving ambidexterity across the product portfolio. The classifications of ambidexterity, in academic literature, have been based on the structure (O'Reilly & Tushman, 2004; Tushman & O'Reilly, 1996) context (Birkinshaw & Gibson, 2004), temporality, etc. individually. However, focus on any one aspect can give misleading results when analyzing NPI at Tata Motors. Rather, a focus on the metaroutine and its impact on shaping the ambidexterity question offer a more robust understanding of the balance between exploration and exploitation.

In summary, metaroutines offer a different approach to ambidexterity when compared to known forms of ambidexterity.

References

Adler, P., Goldoftas, B., & Levine, D. (1999). Flexibility versus efficiency? A case study of model changeovers in the Toyota Production System. *Organization Science, 10*, 43–68.

Birkinshaw, J., & Gibson, C. (2004). Building ambidexterity in an organization. *MIT Sloan Management Review, 45*(4), 47–55.

March, J. G. (1991). Exploration and exploitation in organizational learning. *Organization Science, 2*, 71–87.

O'Reilly, C. A., & Tushman, M. L. (2004). The ambidextrous organization. *Harvard Business Review, 82*, 74–81.

Palepu, K. G., & Srinivasan, V. (September 18, 2004). *Tata Motors: The Tata Ace.* Case Study, Harvard Business School, 1–21.

Tushman, M. L., & O'Reilly, C. A. (1996). Ambidextrous organizations: Managing evolutionary and revolutionary change. *California Management Review, 38*(4), 8–30.

4   Dynamic capabilities and renewal

The success rate of an organization over the long term depends upon its abilities of how effectively it can exploit the current environment and also how it deploys its current capabilities to develop new competencies in a dynamic environment. Studies of companies reveal that while firms may do a fabulous job in bringing out refinements in their product-market offerings, the same organizations tend to falter when it comes to coming up with development of radically new products and services. And hence the need for organizations to develop the twin capabilities of exploiting current market offerings and exploring future businesses at the same time. How do organizations go about building these twin capabilities called dynamic capabilities? And how can the development of dynamic capabilities be a pathway for a potential source of renewal in organizations?

4.1 Evolution of strategic thinking

Introduction

L&T's expansion strategy has been immensely successful in offering high-technology solutions for development of niche products and services—hitherto the forte of companies like Mitsubishi Heavy Industries, Bechtel, etc. Its meteoric rise to technological preeminence is in part due to its renewed focus on cutting-edge technologies and its ability to acquire new capabilities by leveraging existing competencies.

A rich illustration on L&T is provided in Chapter 6, which details how distinct dynamic capabilities can help a company succeed in both existing and new businesses. The concept of dynamic capability is a powerful lens to understand the processes of "sensing" and "seizing" opportunities as well as the process of building sustainable competitive advantage for firms.

4.2 Capabilities and dynamic capabilities

As many markets emerge and die, companies use resource configurations by development of organizational capabilities and strategic routines. Thus the usage of dynamic capabilities helps a firm to leverage and reconfigure its existing competencies and assets in ways that customers find valuable but competitors find difficult to imitate. Dynamic capabilities help in sensing and seizing opportunities by reallocating resources, which is known as resource configuration. Thus resource configuration helps in leveraging existing competencies or developing new ones. Dynamic capabilities can include processes like product development, developing collaborative alliances, etc. Thus according to Teece, Pisano and Shuen (1997), *dynamic capability* is "the firm's ability to integrate, build, and reconfigure internal and external competences to address rapidly changing environments" (p. 516). The uncertainties caused by globalization and disruptive changes have set enormous challenges on how firms can successfully adapt to the market place. In one of the most significant developments in the field of strategy, the emphasis has shifted from the more prevalent static approaches that existed earlier to that of dynamic capabilities. The idea of core competencies is utilized in the development of dynamic capabilities; however what makes it a challenging issue is that of the role of management in building and deploying core competencies to changing environments. Thus the shift to dynamic capabilities acknowledges that with the ever-evolving market place, firms can have a sustainable footing only if they can reallocate assets and develop new skills.

The patterns of dynamic capabilities are likely to vary with market dynamism. Moderately dynamic markets tend to develop changes incrementally but more frequently along predictable lines. As market boundaries are not blurred, competition is also expected along predictable lines unless some player goes about reconfiguring the entire value net (i.e. competitors, customers, complementers, etc.). Thus dynamic capabilities in such markets can be conceptualized as routines.

In contrast, in highly dynamic markets where industry boundaries are blurred, the manifestation of dynamic capabilities is along a different trajectory. Changes are non-linear and less predictable. Companies use experiential and sometimes unstable processes to create new mechanisms that are adaptive, but with unpredictable outcomes. In these markets, the reliance of dynamic capabilities is less on using just existing knowledge and much more on rapidly creating situation-specific new domains of knowledge that may sometime render past knowledge to be redundant.

It is the ability to leverage, adapt and extend existing competencies that separates dynamic capabilities from other applicable frameworks. Senior management in organizations should have the ability to achieve two critical and challenging tasks. They should have the foresight to accurately sense changes in their competitive landscape, which may include shifts in technology, business models, etc. Also the next critical task is about taking actions on these opportunities and looming threats. These two distinct capabilities are the essence of a firm's survival and prosperity.

Sensing and seizing opportunities—Patanjali Ayurved

At a time when most fast-moving consumer goods (FMCG) companies are still skeptical about a pick-up in consumption resulting in improvement in revenues and profitability, Baba Ramdev-promoted Patanjali Ayurved is eyeing 250 percent revenue growth in FY16, according to a recent Edelweiss Research report (2015).

Coming out of nowhere, Patanjali Ayurved is now India's fastest-growing consumer products brand. Established domestic and global competitors are unnerved by the rocketing sales of its wide range of staples, nutrition, cosmetics and personal care products. The products of Patanjali are so popular that analysts are saying that its 20 billion rupee ($307 million) revenues during the year 2015 could pose a threat to established, age-old Indian consumer brands such as Dabur, Emami and Marico. During the month of April 2015, Kishore Biyani, India's own Sam Walton, got a phone call from Baba Ramdev, the co-founder of Patanjali Ayurved. What they talked about can be gauged from the fact that Biyani made two trips to the Patanjali food park near Haridwar in Uttarakhand in the weeks that followed. The astute Marwari was "bowled over by what he saw:" neat and modern production lines packaging a wide range of FMCGs. He tasted some of the foodstuff produced there and instantly liked it. The affair culminated in a deal during early October 2015 under which Biyani will retail Patanjali's 500 or so products: biscuits, juices, honey, supplements, toiletries and instant noodles which are sold through Patanjali's stores and some multi-brand grocery stores; now they will be available in Biyani's Big Bazaar and Food Bazaar supermarket chains. This deal could be a force multiplier for Patanjali—from Rs 2,020 crore (Rs 20.20 billion) in 2014–2015, it hopes to log a turnover of Rs 5,000 crore (Rs 50 billion) during 2015–2016. During the year 2014–2015 the company made a profit of Rs 316 crore (Rs 3.16 billion).

"There is a great demand for their interesting range of products," said Biyani whose group is targeting 10 billion rupees in sales from Patanjali products during the current year (2015). To compare, Biyani's group sells 13 billion rupees worth of Unilever products annually. "I believe Patanjali will hit 50 billion rupees in revenues this year, double it next year and in the next two–three years, become a Top Three Indian consumer products brand," said Biyani.

In the absence of Nestlé's Maggi noodles in the Indian market, Patanjali took the advantage and launched its own Atta noodles, saying it would also get into health drinks for children with a brand called Powervita, which would compete with the likes of MNC products Bournvita, Complan and Horlicks. This would be backed by packaged foods such as pasta, oats and cornflakes, all domains of foreign companies.

Patanjali Ayurved was established in 2006 as a private limited company and subsequently converted into a public limited company in 2007. According to document available with Care Ratings dated May 2015 the company has three manufacturing units located in Haridwar, Uttrakhand for manufacturing its products, with the retail sale of these products being done through Patanjali Arogya Kendra, Patanjali Chikitsalya, Swadeshi Kendra and more than 177,000 retail outlets spread across the country.

Balakrishna owns a 92 percent stake and the rest are held by an expat Indian couple. Baba Ramdev holds no stake in the company. Despite not being a stakeholder in Patanjali, Ramdev, is available whenever the company needs him—for marketing its products, featuring in ad campaigns or even negotiating deals. His style is personal, conversational. While Balkrishna says he is the managing director of Patanjali, its website says that he is the chairman. That aside, Balkrishna, along with Ram Bharat, Ramdev's brother, manages the affairs of the FMCG enterprise.

The company has about 200 employees in the general manager and above bracket. As a whole, the company has staff strength of about 10,000, including contractual workers. Employees are largely hired through job portals and references. The company also has plans to hire MBAs from premier institutes of the country.

Earlier in August 2015, global brokerage and research house CLSA pegged Patanjali Ayurved to be the most diversified FMCG player in India and bigger than listed players like Jyothy Labs and Emami (see Table 4.1).

Table 4.1 Financial performance of Patanjali Ayurved

Year	Net profit (Rs Cr)	Total income (Rs Cr)
2011–2012	55.89	453.38
2012–2013	91.33	848.56
2013–2014	185.67	1191.14
2014–2015	316.60	2028.03

Source: Care rating rationale, May 2015 and September 2014

The journey from yoga to Ayurveda to FMCG products

As per the company's website, Patanjali Ayurved Ltd is not a company. It is a CONCEPT—a concept that links the rising destiny of millions of rural masses on the one hand and many more suffering the onslaught of the unhealthy urban lifestyle on the other. It is all about economically processing farm produce into daily use consumables ranging from Ayurvedic health supplements to foods and cosmetics and then supplying them largely to the urban world.

During an interview with a journalist, Balkrishna recalls how Patanjali diversified from yoga and Ayurveda into juices, when amla farmers spoke to Ramdev and told him about how they found no market for their produce: "Swamiji [Ramdev] then said that we could make amla juice, a form in which amla was never traditionally consumed." Baba Ramdev believed that he could make the product popular through his yoga classes, especially when his followers trusted his word. The company's first products were Aloe Vera Oil and Amla Juice. There was no market for products like these. Nobody ever thought they would sell.

Product range

Patanjali Ayurved Limited produces quality herbomineral preparations. To monitor quality, the Divya Yog Mandir Trust and Patanjali Yog Peeth grow many endangered herbs on its farmland. The principles of Good Manufacturing Practices (GMP) are rigorously followed in the plant and the company prides itself on being environmentally friendly.

According to Edelweiss Research, Patanjali Ayurved operates in three broad business segments—foods (foods, supplements, digestives, dairy, juices, etc.), FMCG (cosmetics (shampoo, soaps, facewash), home care (detergent cakes, powder, liquid, etc.)) and ayurvedic products (healthcare products for blood pressure, skin diseases, joint pain, etc.). The company clocked a turnover of Rs 2,030 crore (Rs 20.30 billion) in FY15 with an EBITDA (earnings before interest, taxation, depreciation and amortization) of around 20 percent. Growth is being driven by the company's largest-selling product, cow's ghee (expected to be Rs 1,200 crore (Rs 12 billion) in FY16) followed by Dant Kanti and Kesh Kanti. Patanajali also has a robust pipeline of new products. Over FY12–15, Patanjali registered revenue CAGR (compounded annual growth rate) of 64.7 percent. In FY15, of the total sales of Rs 2,030 crore (Rs 20.30 billion), food and cosmetics contributed Rs 800 crore (Rs 8 billion) each, while healthcare products comprised the balance. Besides Patanjali Noodles, new launches in the pipeline include Dant Kanti Advance, Sugar-free Chyawanprash, PowerVita, Sea Buckthorn dietary supplement and powdered hair dye, the Edelweiss report says.

Yoga, Ayurveda and the guru

Patanjali broke into Trust Research Advisory's (TRA) annual Brand Trust Report for the first time in 2015, featuring among the seven most trusted Ayurveda brands in the country. TRA Chief Executive N. Chandramouli says this is partly because of Ramdev's own celebrity status in business and political circuits. The man behind the company's meteoric rise is Ramdev, who left his home at the age of 9 to study Sanskrit and yoga. He partnered with "Acharya" Balkrishna in the 1990s to manufacture medicines. Ramdev took the responsibility of popularizing yoga, while Balkrishna focused on the product-side. "Ramdev was also the only spiritual leader to figure in our top 21 personalities list, at number 16 this year. This is the first time in the four years since we launched the report that a spiritual leader has featured on our personality list, otherwise dominated by Bollywood and cricket players," says Chandramouli.

Swadeshi—connecting with the masses

The word swadeshi means self-sufficiency through domestic availability. Thus swadeshi is often understood to mean development of local capabilities to meet local requirements. "We want to create a situation in which multinationals are unable to sell anything in India despite their best efforts to do so. We are hoping to give them a headache," Baba Ramdev said at the conference to announce the deal with Biyani. "Indians should consume Indian products. Why should we allow multinationals to profit at our expense?" It was Biyani's swadeshi roots that led Baba Ramdev to tie up with the man often called India's retail king. Mr. Biyani is the chief executive of Future Group. Not having a business plan does not mean the duo lack ambition. "In five years, I will take swadeshi products of Patanjali to such great heights that foreign companies will dwarf in front of them," declares Ramdev. That's no empty threat. Patanjali will focus on six big product portfolios to drive its growth: a breakfast range including cornflakes, "healthy" noodles, ghee, Kesh Kanti (hair care products), Dant Kanti (oral care products), which is already in the Rs 250 crore (Rs 2.5 billion) range, and Chyawanprash (a cooked mixture of sugar, honey, ghee, Indian gooseberry, jam, sesame oil, berries and various herbs and spices).

Product quality with zero waste, innovation and the cost structure

The product plans are based on identifying products in the market that Patanjali can produce at a lower cost. There is a research facility, with over 50 scientists, which focuses on finding such products.

At the food park that is spread over 150 acres and located 25 km from the Patanjali Yogpeeth, nearly 6,000 liters of amla juice is produced every hour. For such a large output, the food park has a warehouse that spans 100,000 square feet and can store up to 11,500 tonnes of goods. This is also a zero-waste plant. There is a dedicated bio-research institute at Patanjali that works toward how organic waste can be used as fuel, fertilizer and fodder for cattle. The production lines are automated and comparable to the best in the country.

The company's key strength, apart from its superior product quality, Edelweiss says, lies in pricing. The company's products are priced at around 15 percent–30 percent discount to the competition, which makes it an attractive proposition for consumers. Moreover, it is able to offer such discounts primarily because of having negligible Advertising & Promotion (A&P) spend versus other consumer companies that have A&P spends ranging from 12–18 percent, as a percentage of sales. Experts believe that this has been possible through its strong sourcing back-end.

Explaining the 15 percent profit margin, Balkrishna says it is because Patanjali's administrative cost is only up to 2.5 percent of revenue, as against 10 to 15 percent in large companies. "Our top management does not take any money and this helps us scale up our operations while keeping costs low," he says.

In one of the interviews with media personnel, Mr. Balkrishna has said that the company has never done any market research or market survey and that they had focused all their efforts on R&D, product development and quality control; that they never think of commercial benefits and the company's efforts are guided by consumer demand.

We surround ourselves with people and understand their sentiments, needs and desires. For example, the company started selling Aloe Vera Oil at as little as Rs 200 when most MNC priced their product at around Rs 1,300. The company focus was never on the size of the market, but on the demands of the people.

Seeing the aggressive pricing many of the other home grown FMCG companies have dropped prices.

Source: Compiled from various sources

References

Patanjali Ayurved. (2015). *Edelweiss Research report*. Retrieved from www. edelresearch.com/showreportpdf-30172/PATANJALI_AYURVED_-_ VISIT_NOTE-OCT-15-EDEL

Teece, D. J., Pisano, G., & Shuen, A. (1997). Dynamic capabilities and strategic management. *Strategic Management Journal, 18*(7), 509–533.

5 Achieving successful strategic transformation

5.1 Identifying change needs and preparing the organization for change

Broadly defined, organization context encompasses the legitimate systems that exist, the processes that are followed and beliefs that shape individual level behaviors in an organization. Organization context has important similarities to the related concepts of contextual structural elements, culture pertaining to an organization and organization climate that exists. Structural context refers to the establishment of administrative mechanisms that foster certain behavior in employees, but its emphasis is on relatively tangible systems and processes such as incentives or career management systems. Organization culture tends to signify the underlying values and beliefs of individuals in an organization, rather than the established formal systems, structures and processes. Similar views propounded by organization climate researchers have been mentioned to be the encompassing presentation of organizational stimuli or environmental characteristics presumed to affect individual behavior and attitudes.

According to Ghoshal and Bartlett (1994), organizational context is defined in terms of four behavior framing attributes: discipline; stretch; support; and trust. These four attributes are manifested in the various levels and in the various tasks undertaken by managers in a business unit. Through *discipline*, establishment of clear standards of performance and behavior is sought. When employees are driven to achieve more ambitiously driven objectives it signifies *stretch*. Thus through a vision of a shared ambition, and collective identity, members in an organization can stand up to the establishment of stretch. Through *support* members lend assistance to other fellow members. Administrative mechanisms that allow associates to access resources, freedom of initiative and empowerment at lower levels, and senior functionaries giving priority to providing guidance and help rather than to exercising authority, contribute to the establishment of stretch. *Trust* is an attribute of organizational context wherein associates rely on the commitments of each other. Thus fairness and equitable behavior in a business unit's decision processes, and involvement of individuals in decision-making activities contribute to the manifestation of trust.

Ghoshal and Bartlett (1994) conceptualized these four attributes— discipline, stretch, support and trust—as interdependent. An organization, they argued, needs to foster discipline and stretch to encourage individuals to push for realistic stretchable goals, but the same needs to be balanced by building support and trust within a cooperative environment. Organization context, in other words, can be conceptualized in terms of "the yin and yang of continuous self-renewal" (Ghoshal & Bartlett, 1997, p. 151), signifying the balance between hard and soft elements. Ghoshal and Bartlett (1994) did not argue explicitly that these contextual features will develop the capacity for contextual ambidexterity development, but described discipline, stretch, support and trust as engendering individual level behaviors that result in initiative, cooperation and learning. But according to them, individuals take these actions of their own volition and this results in development of ambidexterity which is contextual in nature and which subsequently enhances performance. Evidence from the qualitative interviews conducted by the author with members of various business units of different industries supports these ideas.

In a business unit of a manufacturing firm, until 1998, employees had viewed the company in question as a benevolent employer and a secure place, with an informal culture. However over the last four to five years, a number of changes were brought about, primarily through top–down initiatives revolving around cost reduction and improvement of quality, and through greater focus on key strategic objectives and personal commitment to those objectives. One respondent commented that this business unit was run as a "regimental type organization—appraisal and evaluation interviews are run in a systematic objective driven across business and functional levels and compensation is aligned to reward employees with focus on short-term objectives." Most of these renewal mechanisms were driven by a new executive team that gave people a responsive structure, which further led to refocusing on new products and new opportunities as a means of delivering on the more ambitious goals. The net result was that the imposition of greater discipline, and more top–down direction, generated greater adaptability, whereas before the unit had been evolving in a relatively aimless fashion.

As a second example, in one of the largest petrochemicals units in the Indian oil and gas industry, the organization context was clearly very balanced, and it worked in an autonomous or bottom–up manner. Their "loose tight" model ensured that stretch and discipline were built into performance targets. Trust and support emerged in a subtle way. For example, trust emerged through tangible examples of individuals *not* being punished for well-intentioned failures in projects. Thereafter support was demonstrated with the use of IT systems to increase knowledge of what was happening in other parts of the business, and various forums and councils for cooperating and sharing best practices. Where a lower level of ambidexterity was observed there was evidence that the organization contexts were having weak scores.

Inherent to the research project undertaken by the author from its beginning was the argument that as key leaders in organizations, senior executives play a critical role—because they put in place systems that allow supportive contexts to emerge—that in turn shape individual behaviors (Burgelman, 1983; Ghoshal & Bartlett, 1994). Certainly the research study has found some evidence for this construct (for instance, in the oil and gas business unit and also in manufacturing). However, it is difficult to be too prescriptive, because while the Ghoshal and Bartlett's (1994) framing suggested a common language centered around self-discipline, stretch goals, organization support and trustworthy actions, the reality in the business units in our sample was that each used its own suitable implementation strategy to create a performance management system and social context conducive to the simultaneous achievement of alignment and adaptability. Building on the work of Denison, Hooijberg and Quinn (1995) and others, our results suggest the importance of transcending the either/or of performance management and social context to develop simultaneous abilities of alignment and adaptability.

5.2 The role of leadership

From the dawn of civilization, leadership has been evident in every aspect of human development and progress. Manu or Moses, Ashoka or Alexander are all illustrations of this; epics of all civilizations have innumerable examples of leadership to cite. Humans, from the days they could think and analyze, have been looking at the phenomenon of leadership with awe and for inspiration. Leadership has its own contextual element: it varies from time to time, from culture to culture and from civilization to civilization. The leadership that was prevalent in the feudal societies had certain unique characteristics; leadership styles observed in the same society at different times are bound to be different. Leadership styles have definitely been impacted upon by societal values, technological resources available to the society and the structure of the organizations. Leadership in the context of organizations, in their pursuit of success and achievement of goals is the concern of strategic leadership.

In the article, "Strategic leadership: The function and contribution of CEOs to success in modern business practice," the authors Miah, Gaughan and Wallmann (2002) contend that the main function of the leader is to empower others in the organization. To empower people, the leader has to tap the positive side of the people's emotional energy. To achieve this he/she needs to be clear about the mission of the organization and he/she must be willing to allow the development of the people around him/her. Through this process of human capital development, the leader unleashes a tremendous amount of energy into the organization, which automatically achieves much more than actually intended by the leader. The leader's job is to nurture and unleash the positive energy among the people around him/her; achieving the goals will be done by the people around him/her.

Noel Tichy, seasoned by the GE and the Crotonville experience, argues that long-term sustenance of a firm depends on its ability to nurture leaders from within continuously. The big pictures of leadership best practices go into tactical level details of implementation to achieve the goals. There are six key elements in the leadership engine: teaching; learning; ideas; values; energy; and edge. He also states that the best leaders are enablers rather than doers. They work through others and they are great at empowering the people around them. A true leader, according to him, prepares the firm to win in the short term and to be stronger in the long term.

The book, *The individualized corporation* (Ghoshal & Bartlett, 1997) recognized a major shift from the traditional organization-man to a new invigorating management philosophy that the individual is the core and the key driver of value-creation in the firm and all other aspects surround the core. Some of the key characteristics of the firm are: (1) the ability to inspire creativity and initiative in its people; (2) the ability to link and leverage nuclei of individual expertise into a system of organizational learning; and (3) the ability to continuously renew itself. The managerial implication of this new philosophy is a transformation from the traditional approach of strategy–structure–system to a new approach of purpose–process–people. The firm is perceived not as just an economic entity but as a significant social institution creating new values for all of its constituencies. The roles of the top management and the CEO are redefined in this context.

How does a business leader create an organization that can stand up to the dynamic situations of the competitive world? There are three essential aspects. The vision of the firm must be aligned with the activities of the people. Misalignments have to be identified and corrected; new alignments have to be created. The second aspect is empowerment of the people. People have to be perceived not as assets of the firm but as fountainheads of potential growth. The third aspect is developing a culture of learning across all levels of the organization. This gain is a reflection of what Noel M. Tichy has prescribed in *The leadership engine* (1997).

How does a leader bring a firm out of the trough? In preparing the firm for recovery, the CEO's first task is to create a genuinely compelling vision for the firm. The second task is to communicate this vision to everybody in the firm. This vision must be rock-solid and also very convincing to all in the firm. This is the toughest task because, at this time, none in the firm has a mindset to believe in an upswing or recovery, it is only the convincing power of the CEO that can make the difference. The third task is to pay attention to the best performers. They are the nuclei around which the critical mass gathers for transformation. To accelerate the uptrend, the leader must identify and ensure that the best performers begin the process of nucleation.

A remarkable turnaround is that of Nissan in a fiercely competitive environment. In fact Carlos Ghosn was deputed to Nissan by Renault who had taken over the ailing company. The Nissan story is one of the most brilliant turnaround stories of all time and the credit goes singularly to Carlos Ghosn. Jack Welch, synonymous with GE, offers the classic example of a strategic leader who transformed an aging second-wave manufacturing company into a highly profitable, knowledge-based wealth-churning, third-wave service-sector company.

Strategic leaders unleash highly productive organizational energy inherent in their organizations, thereby creating a strong collective force that fuels purposeful action-taking and leads to extraordinary results.

How did these leaders do it? For one thing they brought the organization together around specific strategic initiatives. In the book, *A bias for action*, Bruch and Ghoshal (2004) mention this to be a two-step process: first mobilizing the organization's energy and then focusing it. At the same time, these leaders appreciated that no company can exist in a state of permanent acceleration, continually striving for higher and higher levels of organizational energy. These leaders succeeded because they carefully nurtured their organization's energy in a way that their people could sustain it steadily over time.

Take for example the way Sony used this strategy to inspire employees toward a new vision. In the early twenty-first century few companies underwent as many fundamental changes as Sony did. Historically a producer of analog-technology-based, standalone audio and video products, Sony was confronting a complete transformation of its businesses. The IT, media and consumer electronics industries were converging to a digitally driven, internet-based, integrated home entertainment business. Accordingly, Sony CEO Noboyuki Idei articulated his vision to enlist the organization in creating a new kind of personal computer. "Young and old alike are truly mesmerized by digital technology. These people, the 'digital dream kids' are our future customers," he said. We must also bring dream kids at all levels of Sony to create something new, something that will meet our future customers' expectations." However no one in the company responded to this first call to action from the CEO. Why? At that time, they did not believe the project could succeed. Sony had already failed twice in its effort to enter the PC business. Even so, Idei did not resort to issuing command-and-control orders. Rather he became a source of inspiration to make the visualization a reality. Idei assigned Kunitake Ando (who later became Sony's Chief Operating Officer (COO)), to create VAIO world, a virtual organization that allowed people to visualize how linking Sony's diverse offerings could exceed the public's future entertainment requirements. VAIO world seduced people into the concept, so those who finally joined in did so as volunteers, because the vision captivated them, not because they got the task.

Thus a gentle, inspiring and empathic style of leaders can unleash passions. It also needs leaders who create an environment of curiosity, excitement and ownership, as Idei did with VAIO world. In this strategy it requires endurance and the ability to cope with and triumph over difficulties. That is why, as a purposeful leader, one must also relentlessly build the company's belief in its ability to realize the shared dream— both by enhancing individual competencies in people and by encouraging and supporting them.
Source: Compiled from various sources

5.3 Tools and techniques for designing and implementing strategic change

Many management teams in organizations are stuck with the paradoxical challenge of how much to exploit in their current core businesses—should they exploit it to their full potential? Or should they be searching for new businesses when the core businesses seem to mature? These questions have baffled management in companies in terms of the timing when to make the next move. In both cases there are examples of companies that have left the core businesses too early or they left it so late that it was almost over. Thus for designing and implementing strategic changes, companies need analytical insights for correctly reading the state of their current businesses and for planning appropriate moves for building the next core.

In a recent influential article in the *Harvard Business Review* titled, "Finding your next core business," Chris Zook (2007), articulates the following critical issues that management in companies need to work out if they are to successfully create a new core (see Table 5.1).

Similarly, while trying to explain "Where does your future lie?" the author tries to explain through three different paths as explained in Table 5.2.

Table 5.1 Critical issues for management to successfully create a new core

Question	Take a close look at
1. What is the state of our core customers?	Profitability Market share Retention rate Measures of nderex loyalty and advocacy Share of wallet
2. What is the state of our core differentiation?	Definition and metrics of differentiation Relative cost position Business models of emerging competitors Increasing or decreasing differentiation
3. What is the state of our industry's profit pools?	Size, growth and stability Share of profit pools captured Boundaries Shifts and projections High costs and prices
4. What is the state of our core capabilities?	Inventory of key capabilities Relative importance Gaps vis-a-vis competitors and vis-a-vis future core needs
5. What is the state of our culture and organization?	Loyalty and undesired attrition Capacity and stress points Alignments and agreements with objectives Energy and motivation Bottlenecks to growth

Table 5.2 Defining future paths

In an undervalued business platform?	In an untapped insight into customers? In an underexpoited capability?	
Undeveloped adjacencies	Unrecognized segments	Hidden corporate capabilities
Organizations that support the core	Privileged access or trust	Non-core capabilities in different divisions
Non-core businesses	Underutilized data and information	Underleveraged core capabilities in different divisions
Orphan products		

Seven steps to a new core business

1. Define the core of your business. Reach consensus on the true state of the core.
2. Assess the core's full potential and the durability of its key differentiation.
3. Develop a point of view about the future, and define the status quo.
4. Identify the full range of options for redefining the core from inside and from the outside.
5. Identify your hidden assets and ask whether they create new options or enable others.
6. Use key criteria (leadership, profit pool, repeatability, chances of implementation) in deciding which assets to employ in redefining your core.
7. Set up a program office to help initiate, track and manage course corrections.

How industries change

Depending upon the trajectory of the industry and how it is changing, the investments that one makes are going to have different pay offs. Industries follow distinctive change trajectories. Investments in innovation are more likely to pay off if one takes those pathways into account (McGahan, 2004). McGahan urges managers in companies to reconsider the core assets and core activities that any firm does and accordingly find out how their core assets/activities have depleted.

What are **core activities?** The recurring actions a company performs that attract and retain suppliers and buyers.

What are **core assets?** The durable resources, including intangibles that make the company more efficient at performing core activities.

The matrix in Figure 5.1 will help managers in revitalizing the core activities and core assets.

Core Assets	Core Activities	
	Threatened	Not threatened
Threatened	**Radical Change** Everything is up in the air Examples: Makers of landline telephone handsets, overnight letter-delivery carriers and travel agencies	**Creative Change** The industry is constantly redeveloping assets and resources Examples: The motion picture industry, sports team ownership and investment banking
Not Threatened	**Intermediate Change** Relationships are fragile Examples: Automobile dealerships, auction houses and investment brokerages	**Progressive Change** Companies adopt incremental testing and adapt to feedback Examples: On line auctions, commercial airlines and long haul trucking

Source: McGahan (2004)

Figure 5.1 Trajectories of industry change

References

Bruch, H., & Ghoshal, S. (2004). A bias for action: How effective managers harness their willpower, achieve results, and stop wasting time. Boston, MA: Harvard Business School Press.

Burgelman, R. A. (1983). A model of the interaction of strategic behavior, corporate context and the concept of strategy. *Academy of Management Review, 8*, 61–70.

Denison, D., Hooijberg, R., & Quinn, R. E. (1995). Paradox and performance: Toward a theory of behavioral complexity in managerial leadership. *Organization Science, 6*, 524–540.

Ghoshal, S., & Bartlett, C. A. (1994). Linking organizational context and managerial action: The dimensions of quality of management. *Strategic Management Journal, 15*, 91–112.

Ghoshal, S., & Bartlett, C. A. (1997). *The individualized corporation: A fundamentally new approach to management*. New York: Harper Business.

McGahan, A. M. (2004). How industries change. *Harvard Business Review, 82*(10), 86–94.

Miah, M., Gaughan, L. K., & Wallmann, J. (2002). Strategic leadership: The function and contribution of CEOs to success in modern business practice. *The CEO Refresher*. Retrieved from www.refresher.com/Archives/!mmjwstrategic.html

Tichy, N. M. with Cohen, E. (1997). *The leadership engine: How winning companies build leaders at every level*. New York: HarperCollins.

Zook, C. (2007). Finding your next core business. *Harvard Business Review, 85*(4), 66–75.

6 Cases of companies undergoing transformation

Case 1: The strategic shift at L&T—from an engineering and construction company to a high-tech engineering driven conglomerate[1]

> We will be a very heavy core-infrastructure builder. We want to be the Indian equivalent of Mitsubishi Heavy Industry.
>
> (Mr. A.M. Naik, CMD of L&T in March 2009, in Shrikant, 2009)

Introduction

On July 3, 2010, the inauguration of the world class terminal-3 (T3) at Indira Gandhi International Airport in Delhi astonished all. Looking at the infrastructure at the airport one can say that the country stands amongst the modern industrialized nations of the world. Hailing the new terminal as exemplifying India's resolve to bridge fast the infrastructure deficit in the country, Prime Minister Dr. Manmohan Singh said T3 (floor space 480,000 sq. m.) built in just 37 months at a cost of about Rs 10,000 crore (Rs 100 billion) has established new global benchmarks (Kumar, 2010). This terminal was developed by L&T in consultation with various foreign players.

Earlier in 2009, L&T made the world take note with its association with the launch of India's first nuclear submarine "Arihant." L&T was involved in a major way in the construction of Arihant since 1998 based on the design supplied by DRDO. L&T being a private player, it was an extraordinary attempt to foray into the development of India's first nuclear submarine project. Though it did not make any money in these projects, it was successful in showcasing its involvement in defense projects with its engineering capabilities. In the same year L&T made investments into nuclear power projects in India. For outside defense contractors who are looking to enter India, these are demonstrations of the capabilities and readiness of the company as a potential partner in any defense business that they might get from the armed services. The joint venture with US defense contractor EADS is an early pointer (Hindu Business Line, 2011). L&T further showed its technical prowess and brilliance with its involvement in an underwater surveillance mechanism leading to the development of "Nagan" to enhance an anti-submarine warfare program. As we mentioned earlier, the investments made are not just about pursuing growth opportunities. They also signify a strategic shift—from being an engineering and construction services company to a hi-tech high-end engineering driven conglomerate.

Background note

The evolution of L&T into the country's largest engineering and construction company is among the most remarkable success stories in Indian industry. L&T was founded in Bombay (Mumbai) in 1938 by two Danish engineers, Henning Holck-Larsen and Soren Kristian Toubro. Both of them were strongly committed to developing India's engineering capabilities to meet the demands of industry before Independence. Beginning with the import of machinery from Europe, L&T rapidly took on engineering and construction assignments of increasing sophistication. On February 7, 1946, Larsen & Toubro Private Limited was born with the intention to raise additional equity capital for buying a large number of war-surplus caterpillar equipment which was available at attractive prices. This was a golden opportunity as L&T was already in an agreement with Caterpillar Tractor Company, U.S.A. for marketing earth moving equipment since 1945.

After India achieved Independence and the subsequent demand for technology and expertise offered L&T the opportunity to consolidate and expand, offices were set up in Kolkata (Calcutta), Chennai (Madras) and New Delhi. In 1948, 55 acres of undeveloped marsh and jungle was acquired in Powai. Today, Powai stands as a tribute to the vision of the men who transformed this uninhabitable swamp into a manufacturing landmark. In December 1950, L&T became a public company with a paid up capital of Rs 2 million. The sales turnover in that year was Rs 10.9 million. Prestigious orders executed by the company during this period included the Amul Dairy at Anand and Blast Furnaces at Rourkela Steel Plant. With the successful completion of these jobs, L&T emerged as the largest erection contractor in the country.

In 1956, a major part of the company's Bombay office moved to ICI House in Ballard Estate. A decade later this imposing gray-stone building was purchased by L&T and renamed as L&T House—its corporate office. The 1960s saw a significant change at L&T—S.K. Toubro retired from active management in 1962. The 1960s were also a decade of rapid growth for the company, and witnessed the formation of many new ventures: UTMAL (set up in 1960); Audco India Limited (1961); Eutectic Welding Alloys (1962); and TENGL (1963). By 1964, L&T had widened its capabilities to incorporate usage of the best technologies in the world. In the decade that followed, the company grew rapidly, and by 1973 had become one of the Top-25 Indian companies. In 1976 Holck-Larsen was awarded the Magsaysay Award for International Understanding in recognition of his contribution to India's industrial development. He retired as chairman in 1978.

In the decades that followed, the company grew into an engineering major under the guidance of leaders like N.M. Desai, S.R. Subramaniam, U.V. Rao, S.D. Kulkarni and A.M. Naik. The 1980s and 1990s saw rapid expansion across all divisions. L&T slowly went on to become one of India's biggest and best known industrial houses with a reputation for technological excellence, high quality of products and services and strong customer orientation.

L&T toward the end of the twentieth century

Toward the end of the twentieth century L&T was a conglomerate broadly having three business segments—Engineering and Construction (ECC), Electrical Business Group (EBG) and Cement. The unfocused business segments of L&T were glass, tractors, cement. None of the businesses were unprofitable, but the recommendations given by BCG (Boston Consulting Group) in 1999 made them sit up and take notice. BCG recommended that L&T focus on core areas of its strength and leverage its engineering skills to get into new businesses where competitive barriers were high.

L&T at the beginning of the twenty-first century

In order to reposition itself, L&T implemented three consecutive five year plans from 2000. L&T thereafter divested its unrelated businesses of cement, glass and tractors in its first five year plan operational during 2000–2005. A nation's progress is measured in terms of its basic infrastructure, i.e. telecommunication, transportation and electricity. L&T's vision was to focus on the development of the latter two. It widened its arena of business by entering into shipbuilding, power projects, metro rail, highways and defense. This zeal of L&T was not limited to building its image in India; it gained great respect in terms of remarkable execution of any overseas project. With this unmatched ambition, L&T paved its way to become a high-technology value engineering company from an unfocused diversified conglomerate.

The engineering and construction industry overview

The engineering industry accounts for 12 percent of India's GDP.[2] The Indian engineering sector is broadly categorized into two segments—heavy engineering and light engineering. The engineering sector is relatively less fragmented at the top, as the competencies required are high, while it is highly fragmented at the lower end and is dominated by smaller players. Most of the leading players are engaged in the production of high value products using high-end technology. Requirement of high level of capital investment poses a major entry barrier. Consequently, the small and unorganized firms have a small market presence. The major end-user for heavy engineering goods are power, infrastructure, steel, cement, petrochemicals, oil & gas, refineries, fertilizers, mining, railways, automobiles, textiles, etc. Light engineering goods are essentially used as inputs by the heavy engineering industry. Several new projects being undertaken in various core industries such as railways, power, infrastructure, etc. are reasons behind growth in the Indian engineering sector.

India enjoys a cost advantage in casting and forging as manufacturing cost in India is 25–30 percent lower than western countries ("Auto part cos.," 2007). The Engineering Service Outsourcing (ESO) sector is another sector with great potential. ESO includes product design, research, development and other technical services across sectors. According to ratings agency Fitch, India is one of the largest and most dynamic infrastructure and project finance markets in the world. The infrastructure sector accounts for 26.7 percent of India's industry.[3] Government initiatives like the National Highway Development project and the National Maritime Development program have given thrust to infrastructure projects. The Indian construction industry encompasses establishments engaged in building residential, commercial and civil engineering works. This industry segment includes residential, farm, industrial, commercial or other buildings constructed by general contractors and operative builders. The main industrial growth drivers are increased spending on infrastructure projects and increased non-residential development (refer to Table 6.1).

Table 6.1 Current share of businesses in L&T's turnover

Business segment	Share in total (%)	Order booked (%)
Infrastructure	39	41
Hydrocarbons	12	14
Power	25	22
Process	16	16
Others	08	07

Source: Annual Report-2010

Table 6.2 Detailed offerings of L&T

Construction	Infrastructure projects, buildings and factories, power transmission and distribution projects, realty project
Engineering products and Systems	Refinery, oil and gas, petrochemicals, fertilizer, coal gasification, aerospace, thermal power plants, nuclear power plant, defense
Electrical and electronic products & systems	Switchgear products, electrical systems, metering solutions, medical equipment and systems, control and automation
IT and engineering services	IT services, integrated engineering services
Machinery & industrial products	
Financial services	Equipment finance, infrastructure finance, general insurance, mutual fund, portfolio management service

L&T's product portfolio

As of 2011, L&T is an Indian conglomerate that has presence in many areas of the globe with specific focus on the domestic market and the Middle East. L&T's product portfolio includes engineering products and systems, construction, power, electrical & electronics, machinery & industrial products, IT & engineering services, financial services and turnkey projects. (Refer to Table 6.2 for detailed offerings of L&T.) L&T's heavy engineering division lays claim to be among the top five fabrication companies in the world. It supplies custom designed and engineered critical equipment as per the needs of the core industrial and defence sector. L&T has a dedicated subsidiary—Engineering, Construction and Contracts (ECC) division for construction business. L&T Power is an independent unit under L&T that deals in opportunities in coal-based, gas-based and nuclear power projects. This division provides support for setting up utility power plants, cogeneration and captive power plants.

Competitive positioning[4]

L&T is a conglomerate that represents a classic example of resource-based theory of strategy (Grant, 1991) formulation. L&T successfully utilized its resources (engineering skills) to gain capabilities thus culminating into competitive advantage for the group. In formulating its strategy for having a sustainable competitive advantage that competitors cannot imitate easily, L&T placed strong emphasis on learning by virtue of various collaborations and consultations. It is one organization in India that has actually been quite successful at both exploiting the present and exploring the future opportunities. It has found a way to maintain organization separation of its traditional businesses and new exploratory ventures. It thus exhibits characteristics of an "ambidextrous organization" (O'Reilly & Tushman, 2004). The strength and weakness analysis of L&T for the time period 2005 to 2010 is summarized below.

Strengths

Market leadership

L&T is one of the largest and most respected groups in India and unlike many of its competitors is not a family owned business but professionally managed with modest international presence and has a well-planned strategy. A detailed analysis in the present engineering and construction industry landscape has enabled the conglomerate to adopt a strategic posture for diversification—a strategy based on market share, scale of operations, ability to differentiate and preemption of competitors. The group is leveraging its strong brand name to gain competitive advantage for expansion into international markets.

Diverse range of products and services

L&T offers a diverse range of products and services. The group is active in six business segments namely engineering & construction, electrical and electronics, machinery and industrial products, financial services, development projects and others. Such a diverse portfolio of products and services allows L&T to record steady revenues and huge selling opportunities.

Unmatched project management skills and technical expertise

L&T owns engineering design research centers in various parts of India and abroad to include feasibility studies, project reports, system engineering, architecture and structural design for infrastructure development projects.

Focus on learning through partnering

Being associated with some of the big brand name partners like Mitsubishi, Atomstroyexport, etc. has enabled L&T to develop capabilities in many fields. This shows the foresightedness of L&T to learn and develop capabilities before execution.

Cost control

L&T's project management skills enable the company to complete projects ahead of schedule, which in turn results in saving costs and working capital. Reduced redundancies and rework elimination help L&T to reuse proven concepts that reduce the cost of designs and prototype development.

Weaknesses

Dependence on domestic operations

L&T is more dependent on domestic operations for its revenue growth. Although the company has turnkey projects in UAE and other gulf countries, it accounts for a small portion of the group's overall operations. The effect of business cycles in the domestic market may affect L&T revenues and profitability.

Leadership vacuum

L&T has grown so far under the leadership of Mr. A.M. Naik. L&T today is a result of Naik's foresightedness and vision. The company will face a temporary vacuum in the absence of the unmatched leadership skills of Mr. Naik.

Substantial amount of debt

The nature of the turnkey projects that L&T operates requires a lot of investment; profits come only after the entire project is successfully executed. In such circumstances managing the debt burden is difficult.

Competitors and L&T

Within heavy engineering, L&T's main competitors are engineering companies like Samsung, Bechtel Corporation, Hyundai Engineering, National Petroleum Construction Company (NPCC) and Engineers India. Within the construction space its main competitors are Punj Lloyd, Gammon India, Hindustan Construction company (HCC), Nagarjuna Construction company (NCC), DLF, GMR, Tata Power, etc.

The strategic shift

Prior to its transformation until the end of the 1990s, L&T was widely perceived as an unfocused company with interests in several areas such as cement, tractors and glass which coexisted with its core expertise in engineering and construction. As a result of its strategic evaluation made by Boston Consulting Group in 1999, the company decided to concentrate on high value engineering and infrastructure segments.

Phases of transformation

Moving to high-tech business

Since the year 2000, restructuring has been a part of L&T culture. The overall restructuring includes the creation of a new focused organization structure to enhance transparency, accountability and management focus. The conglomerate initiated its transformation process through the implementation of three consecutive five year plans beginning from 2000. L&T then decided to focus itself on larger scale projects like airport, roads, ports, oil exploration & refineries, aerospace and defence (Rathi, 2006) to harness its engineering capabilities.

Phase 1: 2000–2005

In line with its first restructuring plan, L&T had divested its cement business in favor of the Aditya Birla Group and its ready-mix concrete business in favor of Lafarge SA. In order to get rid of its non-core businesses, L&T sold its 17 million tonne cement business to Grasim under the Aditya Birla flag in the year 2004. The cement business contributed 27 percent of the gross revenue for the year 2002–2003 (Banerjee & Diwedi, 2009). By 2005, the other business division that L&T closed was its glass business. After undergoing proposals from various buyers for two years, L&T sold its glass container business to

Ace Glass Containers of CK Somani Group. By the end of its first five year plan in July 2005, L&T exited the tractor business by divesting its stake in its joint venture, L&T–John Deere Private Ltd. L&T had made an investment of Rs 87.5 crore (Rs 0.875 billion) in this venture which lasted for almost ten years, i.e. from 1997 to 2005. The venture remained profitable until its end.

The Chairman of L&T, Mr. A.M. Naik said this divestment, as well as the demerger and planned sale of the cement division to Grasim, is in keeping with the Boston Consulting Group's advice to the company to exit from all its non-core areas. Mr. Naik described the core areas of the company as construction, projects, heavy engineering, machinery, then electronics and electrical, information technology and information technology enabled services (ITES). "IT is a growth area for us," he said ("L&T to exit," 2003). The BCG plan which was drawn up until the year 2005 is being followed by another five year plan for L&T up to year 2009–2010.

Phase 2: 2005–2010

In 2008, L&T started to tap the nuclear power opportunity ahead by firming up its forging plans. L&T made an investment of Rs 2,000 crore (Rs 20 billion) in establishing a forging plant at Hazira. In August 2009, L&T had announced an internal restructuring exercise wherein it planned to form a new entity within the company to cater to the growing opportunities within the railway sector. The new entity was to be formed from L&T's existing arms which were currently involved in railway work including the manufacturing, design and marketing arms. The company had also announced plans to enter the general insurance business.

In 2009 L&T signed a memorandum of understanding (MOU) with Atomstroyexport (ASE) of Russia for cooperation between the two companies for Russian design reactors VVER 100. The MOU formed the basis of cooperation between the companies to address needs for equipment and other services arising from the agreement signed between India and Russia in 2008.

Phase 3: 2010–2015

L&T had played a leading role in equipment manufacture, construction and project management for pressurized heavy water reactors in India's domestic nuclear program.

L&T sensed the opportunity of $1.5 billion (Rs66.9 billion)) annual business from nuclear power in another three to five years. The company realized that a major part of the growth in this business had to come from nuclear power producers outside India. "A number of reactors in these countries would go for replacements of some of the parts and upgrades. That would be an opportunity L&T will be looking at," said M. V. Kotwal, President, Heavy Engineering. As a part of its heavy engineering division, the company manufactures vessels for pressurized heavy water reactors, fast breeder reactors, steam generator assemblies, heat transport systems and other critical equipment. Thus the company got engaged in engineering, procurement and construction of nuclear power plants. To strengthen its hold on nuclear business, L&T formed a joint venture with Nuclear Power Corporation of India Ltd (74:26 percent).

Thereafter for L&T there was no looking back. The company takes the credit for the installation of huge refineries and petrochemical complexes having built the world's largest continuous catalyst regenerator, the world's longest LPG pipeline, the world's largest cross-country conveyor, Asia's highest viaduct and the country's first indigenous hydrocracker reactor. L&T's vision is to become a $12 billion global behemoth by 2015 and has an audacious plan to be ranked amongst the top players like Bechtel, Technip and JPC. Mr. Naik commented on this ambitious plan:

> We want to ensure through our initiative that in 2015, we look like a company with a strong high-end construction and infrastructure building ability along with programme management capabilities that no one in India has today. By the end of that period, we would have moved up the value chain tremendously. Each vertical that we operate in would be bigger than $1 billion in size.
>
> (Rathi, 2006)

In order to accomplish its vision the company aims to break out of its traditional geographical markets and penetrate the US and European markets (where it is acquiring front-end companies that offer cutting edge technologies and know-how).

How L&T preempts its competitors

1. Seizing domestic opportunities like huge demand in infrastructure arising out of the public expenditure program on the government's agenda.
2. Entering into zones where entry barriers are high.
3. Partnering with technological giants to learn technological skills through which it reaps huge benefits.

4. Extension of geographical arena to emerge as an excellent company on the global level.
5. Continuously sensing and seizing opportunities for growth.

The capability build up journey

In line with its strategic dictate, L&T has made huge investments in people, processes and financing projects to build capabilities in the following businesses:

- In its shipbuilding facility at Kattupalli in Tamil Nadu, L&T has invested Rs 3,000 crore (Rs 30 billion). The face of Kattupalli has been registering a remarkable change with the investment L&T has made in constructing a shipyard, a modular fabrication facility and a container port. L&T had employed 3,000 workers in building this sprawling complex spread over 1,200 acres. The shipyard incorporates state of the art design and engineering features. The Kattupalli shipyard will initially build defense related ships and later will be used for commercial shipbuilding and ship repairs. L&T has received orders for coastguard ships. Initial capacity of two container berths at Kattupalli would be 1.2 million TEUs (20 foot equivalent unit of a container) (Vishwanathan, 2011, p. 30).

- Investments of Rs 1,700 crore (Rs 17 billion)in supercritical boilers have been made and appropriately L&T has formed a joint venture with Mitsubishi Industries Limited for the setting up of a manufacturing facility for supercritical boilers. The purpose of this alliance is technology transfer and licensing agreement. Manufacturing capabilities for supercritical boilers integrates L&T's existing strength in the power sector. Supercritical boilers will bridge the demand and supply gap of power plant equipment in India and help in boosting power generation capabilities ("L&T, Mitsubishi," 2007).

- In 2008, L&T started to tap into the nuclear power opportunity by firming up its forging plans. The MOU with Atomstroyexport (ASE) of Russia formed the basis of cooperation between the companies to address needs for equipment and other services arising from the agreement signed between India and Russia in 2008 for four additional KK3–6 reactors at Kudankulam, Tamil Nadu and other Russian reactors. L&T had played a leading role in equipment manufacture, construction and project management for pressurized heavy water reactors in India's domestic nuclear program. It became the only Indian company to be accredited by ASME (American Society of Mechanical Engineers) to use its "N" and "NPT" stamps for critical nuclear reactor equipment. L&T played an important role in construction, piping and erection services for the KK1–2 VVERs at Kudankulam ("L&T signs MoU," 2009).

The company has aimed to get orders worth Rs 1,500 crore (Rs 15 billion) in the nuclear sector annually. The nuclear business could be worth Rs 7,000 crore (Rs 70 billion) annually if projects on a turnkey basis are allowed. "Let me do the whole thing (nuclear plant) and I will deliver it in five years," Mr. Naik said ("The L&T can build," 2009). He stressed changing the mode of execution of projects from piecemeal to turnkey. Mr. Naik also mentioned that 25 such plants are expected to come up in India in the next two decades. "In the next four years alone, we would have revenues of nearly Rs 2,500 crore [Rs 25 billion] from nuclear power sector" ("The L&T can build," 2009). To strengthen its hold on nuclear business, L&T formed a joint venture with Nuclear Power Corporation of India Ltd (74:26 percent). Being set up with an investment of Rs 1,700 crore (Rs 17 billion), the new L&T–NPCIL facility, one of the seven L&T plants, would be a fully integrated plant—covering the entire range on a turnkey basis, from melting of steel to finished equipment—under the public–private partnership (PPP) model to indigenously produce special steels and ultra-heavy forgings for nuclear reactors, pressurizers and steam generators, in addition to heavy forgings for critical equipment in the hydrocarbon sector as well as for thermal power plants.

For defense contracts, the company has showcased its capabilities by contributing to the construction of India's first advanced technology vessel "Arihant" and "Nagan." What L&T had tried to display by getting involved in defense projects that had not brought any money to the company, was its capability to be seen as the potential partner for defense contracts. Larsen & Toubro and Cassidian (new name of EADS Defence & Security) have joined forces in the field of defense electronics. The joint venture, based in Talegaon near Pune and in Bangalore, will be active in the defense electronics market. It aims to cover manufacturing, design, engineering, distribution and marketing in the fields of electronic warfare, radars, avionics and mobile systems (such as bridges) for military applications. The joint venture will cooperate closely with Cassidian's new engineering center in Bangalore where systems design and engineering activities will be carried out in the fields of electronic warfare, radars and avionics for military application. The new joint venture will deliver indigenous solutions for military requirements of India as well as the world market. Thus, the Indian joint venture will provide the armed forces with locally produced high-tech equipment and assured life-time support.

Recognizing L&T's growing engineering engagements established with EADS Tier-I suppliers, EADS Group Procurement signed a contract with L&T. This agreement will also enable L&T to be part of EADS strategic programs. M.V. Kotwal, Member of the Board and L&T President, Heavy Engineering said:

> In addition to its other businesses, L&T has been a leading company in India for engineering, manufacture & integration of custom made technology intensive equipment and systems. The coming together of L&T with Cassidian, the defense, electronics & security arm of the European defense & aerospace company—EADS, is a major shot in the arm in the area of defense electronics. It will not only serve the Indian armed forces with state-of-the art technology, but also provide a platform for making significant contributions to the global market in high-technology defense equipment.
>
> ("L&T and Cassidian," 2010)

Cassidian is a high-tech company supporting global security by the development of high-tech product and system solutions for armed forces and civil security worldwide.

On the tie up with L&T, Mr. Bernd Wenzler, CEO Cassidian Electronics ("L&T and Cassidian," 2010) said,

> We are proud of joining forces with one of India's biggest technology companies. Our joint venture is proof of our commitment to India. Cassidian would like to establish an Indian industrial base for our European technologies with the development of a long term partnership. We are prepared to bring additional capabilities into the JV Company after the Indian laws allow an increase of shares up to 49 percent.
>
> ("L&T and Cassidian," 2010)

L&T has played a leading role in India's indigenization effort for defense equipment and systems. With an impressive track record that includes design, development and manufacture of integrated multidisciplinary defense systems, L&T has matured into a trusted partner for the Indian Armed Forces and DRDO.

Domestic opportunities

In August 2009, L&T had announced an internal restructuring exercise wherein it planned to form a new entity within the company to cater to the growing opportunities from the railway sector. The new entity was to be formed from L&T's existing arms, which were currently involved in railway work, including the manufacturing, design and marketing arms. The construction of 71.6 km of Hyderabad metro railway costing Rs 16,500 crore (Rs 165 billion) has been taken up (Vishwanathan, 2011, p. 28). Besides Hyderabad metro rail, L&T is also involved in the construction of sections of Chennai metro rail and three underground stations. All the four modern airports at Hyderabad, Bengaluru, Delhi and Mumbai have been constructed by L&T to tight (schedules and budgets. The Rs 7,000 crore (Rs 70 billion) Delhi airport was made ready well in time for the Commonwealth Games and was the crowning achievement for L&T. The recent major construction job taken by L&T is a 244 km four lane highway costing Rs 2,200 crore (Rs 22 billion) in Rajasthan linking the northern hinterland with the Mundra and Kandla ports in Gujarat. L&T is also involved in development and upgradation of Paradip, Bina and Bhatinda refineries.

How L&T nurtures alliances

A critical skill of L&T right since inception has been to forge and nurture alliances which have helped the company to acquire new capabilities for growth. One critical success factor of the organization can be attributed to its numerous alliances in place in all businesses. Company officials prefer to look at the operating company structure as a portfolio of businesses, rather than a vertical division of activity and labor. The restructuring of the firm got rid of the cement and other non-engineering related businesses and the moves into defense, power and nuclear power are readjustments of the business portfolio. L&T not only builds roads, but owns eight of them under a build, operate and transfer arrangement. "It gives L&T a way of participating in the project either as an owner or a contractor," says the head of infrastructure practice at a consulting firm in Mumbai." A shift in either position just means a readjustment of business portfolio. A similar arrangement was worked for a captive power plant for Haldia Petrochemicals, though it was a small one. L&T took a stake of approximately Rs 100 crore (Rs 1 billion) in the project as it undertook the construction of the power plant, and exited after delivery at a profit. This approach also works with L&T's cashstrapped clients. In 2007, Dubai Aluminum announced a project for building an aluminum-processing plant in Orissa. It invited L&T to take a 26 percent stake in the project for about Rs 3,000 crore (Rs 30 billion). The contract for building and commissioning the plant is worth Rs 7,000 crore (Rs 70 billion) to L&T (Shrikant, 2009). Senior management sees the parts of the portfolio as an extension of scope, rather than as change in scale, which already exists.

Acquiring dynamic capabilities: Promoting ambidexterity

The organizational structure of L&T is complex with 12 operating companies between five and six divisions, many joint ventures and wholly owned subsidiaries. On actual scrutiny it would also be an equivalent of more than 100 small companies in its fold. This complexity raises an important question: is L&T a diversified conglomerate or an integrated one? "The businesses we are in are inherently complex," says J.P. Nayak, President, Machinery and Industrial Products at L&T, who also oversees the company's strategy. "As you would have seen we have moved away from the commodities businesses and from businesses that have low entry barriers. We are an engineering powerhouse, which seeks the kind of complex projects that test our engineering mettle."

L&T manages to retain the benefits of size, especially in marketing and manufacturing. It is no exception when it comes to leveraging its brand power. The group is leveraging its strong brand name to gain competitive advantage for expansion into international markets. According to L&T's former CEO Mr. Kulkarni, "Only through empowerment and decentralized decision-making can a highly diversified company like L&T be managed." Taken together, these processes emphasize strategic insight and execution as well as general management leadership responsibility. While many organizations have several of these elements as a part of their strategy process, what is different about the L&T approach is that they have an integrated set of mechanisms to both sense and seize opportunities. This allows the firm to consider trends in markets and technology, to identify issues that are relevant to customers, to examine them in detail and to reconfigure assets to address them.

The process begins with the recognition that mature, well-established businesses need to operate differently from new, exploratory ones. To succeed, emerging businesses have different key success factors and different styles of leadership and different alignments of people, informal organization systems and culture. L&T recognized that the current management system rewarded short-term execution aimed at current markets. Trying to operate new business within an existing mature one can be exceedingly difficult, with the result that the new business is often killed. Further the company lacked the discipline for selecting, experimenting, funding and terminating new businesses. This led to the development of a process to identify new growth opportunities—all with senior management oversight to ensure that the new businesses get the resources needed to explore the opportunity. The overall process by which L&T operates in terms of acquiring dynamic capabilities can be summed up by the framework in Figure 6.1.

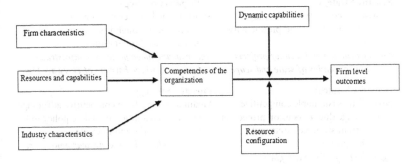

Figure 6.1 A framework of dynamic capabilities at L&T
Source: Developed by the author

The transformation

L&T has been able to shed old uncompetitive businesses, and enter into new businesses by reconfiguring itself and its resource allocation. It has deployed multiple strategies in place for sensing and seizing opportunities, which enables it to acquire dynamic capabilities and create a path for continuous renewal. Please refer to Figure 6.2 for types of strategies employed by L&T.

Amidst all the praise he received for transforming L&T, Naik was also suitably modest and noted that L&T's forte is in engineering. What he tried to do was basically leverage the engineering capabilities L&T possessed into high end areas. Essentially it was about sensing and seizing opportunities wherein L&T could make a significant impact with its engineering excellence.

The real change required was for the company to reallocate assets and to reconfigure itself to be able to compete in a different way. It meant walking away from history and a long standing business model. This required seeing the market place differently. But Naik claimed that L&T already had the right strategies. More importantly, it required a cultural transformation that allowed the company to reconfigure itself and to reallocate resources so that they could execute those strategies. What the transformation of L&T illustrates is that while organizations are often characterized by strong inertial forces that limit change, it is by no means impossible to accomplish change. The key to sustained profitable growth is the ability to recombine and reconfigure assets and organizational structures as markets and technologies change. To accomplish such change, however requires that senior managers be able to not only sense the changes needed by their firms, but also to be able to seize them by allocating resources and reconfiguring the organization

Reactive Strategy	Anticipatory Strategy
Short-term competitive advantage through efficiency and productivity effects *e.g. construction and turnkey projects giving economies of scale and scope*	Short- to medium-term competitive advantage Through first mover advantage and enhanced reputation *e.g. acquiring mega projects in infrastructure businesses where barriers of entry are high*
Defensive Strategy	Proactive Strategy
No or little sustainable competitive advantage due to focus on protection of current strategic assets and market position *e.g. selling off of cement, glass businesses*	Medium-to long-term competitive advantage through redefinition of public policy to fit firm's Strengths and interests *e.g. shipbuilding, defense, nuclear power, etc.*

Figure 6.2 Types of strategies employed by L&T

to address them. This involves seeing things realistically, being willing to cannibalize existing businesses when necessary and being ambidextrous or able to manage both mature and emerging businesses.

Outlook

As exemplified by L&T, acquiring dynamic capabilities offers a source of sustainable competitive advantage. What it translates to is the development of specific strategic and organizational processes like product development; alliancing and strategic decision-making that create value for firms within dynamic markets by manipulating resources into new value-creating strategies. The value for competitive advantage lies in L&T's ability to alter the resource base: create, integrate, recombine and release resources. As L&T looks into the future, the future looks challenging in terms of how it organizes itself to meet the environmental changes. The continual efforts of top management to bring in changes have helped it to acquire new capabilities and it is well positioned to leverage the usage of its capabilities with technology to give the best. As L&T aspires itself to become one of the top five heavy engineering companies of the world, it has to execute more projects worldwide on a global scale. And L&T is well positioned to achieve its objective.

Notes

1 Earlier published by Swarup Kumar Dutta and Pragya Bhawsar (2013) The strategic shift at L&T: From an engineering and construction company to a high-tech engineering driven conglomerate. *International Journal of Business Insights and Transformation,* 6(1), 66–75. Reproduced with permission.

2 Engineering Industry. Introduction.. Retrieved from www.ibef.org/industry/ engineering
3 Infrastructure industry. Retrieved from www.ibef.org/artdisplay.aspx?art_ id=29219&cat_ id=114&page=1
4 Data Monitor, Company Profile, L&T Limited, May 27, 2010.

References

Auto part cos. tap new sectors to drive growth. (2010, April 6). *The Economic Times*. Retrieved from http://articles.economictimes.indiatimes.com/2010-04 06/news/28480836_1_ auto-component-component-makers-ashok-taneja

Banerjee, A., & Diwedi, N. (2009). L&T restructuring the cement business. *Asian Case Research Journal, 9*(1), 83–113.

Grant, R. M. (1991). The resource based theory of competitive advantage: Implications for strategy formulation. *California Management Review, 33*(3), 114–135.

Hindu Business Line, The. (2011, February 10). L&T, EADS form venture for defence electronics equipment. Retrieved from www.thehindubusinessline. com/Companies/article1327607.ece

Kumar, V. (2010). Retrieved from www.thehindu.com/news/cities/Delhi/ article498539

L&T and Cassidian join forces in India to forge a long term partnership. (2010, February 10). *Business Standard*. Retrieved from www.business standard. com/india/news/Ltcassidian-join-forces-in-india-to-forgelong-term-partnership/424701/

L&T to exit 100 crore glass business. (2003, December 29). *The Economic Times*. Retrieved from http://articles.economictimes.indiatimes.com/2003-1229/news/ 27538527_1_cementbusiness- glass-unit-businesses-account

L&T, Mitsubishi heavy industries in JV for super-critical boilers. (2007, April 18). *Financial Express*. Retrieved from www.financialexpress.com/archive/lt-mitsubishi-heavy-ind-in-jv-for-super-critical-boilers/196941/

L&T signs MoU with Atomstrong export for nuclear power reaction. (2009, April 16). *Machinist.In*. Retrieved from http://machinist.in/index. php?option=com_content&task=view&id=2041&Itemid =2

O'Reilly, C. A., & Tushman, M. L. (2004). The ambidextrous organization. *Harvard Business Review, 82*, 74–81.

Rathi, D. (2006, November 20). Core critical. *Outlook*. Retrieved from http:// business.outlookindia.com/article.aspx?100869

Shrikant, S. (2009, August 10). Quantum leap. *Business World*, 30–39.

The L&T can build higher capacity nuclear plant. (2009, September 30). *The Hindu*. Retrieved from www.thehindu.com/business/article26728.ece

Vishwanathan, S. (2011, July). L&T engineers a sea change at Kattupalli. *Industrial Economist*.

Case 2: Eveready Industries: the magic lamp that changed the fortunes[1]

Introduction

Sometime in the mid-summer of 2008, Mr. Deepak Khaitan was feeling restless sitting in his office in Kolkata, India. He was jolted by the fact that the demand for his core battery business was fast declining. This was the same business which had once commanded a domestic market share of 60 percent. Cheap Chinese battery imports to India caused the demand for its best-selling battery to fall from 600 million to 300 million in just one year. But Mr. Khaitan who was the vice chairman and managing director of Eveready Industries Ltd felt that the company's problems were much deeper. On top of its falling domestic demand, the company did not have the license to sell Eveready batteries in many overseas markets. In many overseas markets the brand was owned by Energizer. He had to hit upon a brilliant yet radical way of bolstering the bread and butter business of Eveready Industries. The rapid changes required him to act fast. Deep inside his guts, he understood that it was the most disruptive phase since the Kolkata-based B.M. Khaitan Group company took over Eveready Industries from Union Carbide in 1994.

Born out of sheer necessity of survival, Eveready Industries made its experimental foray of entering the LED (light-emitting diode) lantern (lamp) business (Dubey, 2009). The new business aimed to create a new growth opportunity by catering to the bottom-of-the-pyramid customers of an emerging country like India. The new offering would replace kerosene lanterns in many parts of power-starved states like UP, Bihar, West Bengal, etc. On the other end, this lamp would need batteries to operate on, which would create a further traction for Eveready's existing battery business. Further, if it could be provided at the right price range to be cheaper than traditional kerosene lamps, it would fill a significant void in the Indian market. The experimental foray led to unprecedented success, which changed the fortunes of Eveready from 2009 onwards. At the heart of the LED lanterns business is Eveready's philosophy, "You can live in darkness, but once you are used to light, you will never go back to darkness." This philosophy was built on providing better light at a lower monthly cost than using kerosene lanterns.

What then were the challenges and pitfalls faced by Eveready Industries in taking an alternative growth path born out of adversity? What strategies did it adopt in revitalizing the company?

Background note

The history of Eveready Industries began in 1905 with the starting of the Indian Operations of National Carbon. The first dry cell batteries were imported from the U.S.A. and sold in the major cities of the country. These batteries were primarily used in imported torches. In 1926 National Carbon set up its own subsidiary, Eveready Company in Kolkata, India which was India's first arc carbon factory. In 1934, Eveready Company was incorporated as a private company and the company expanded by setting up the first modern battery plant at Cossipore, Kolkata in 1939. After getting acquired by Union Carbide Corporation, the company was renamed as Union Carbide India Ltd in 1951.

By the time of the Bhopal Disaster in 1984, the company was ranked twenty-first in size among companies operating in India. It had revenues of Rs 2 billion (then equivalent to US$170 million).

In 1995 Union Carbide India Ltd was sold to McLeod Russel, a group company of Williamson Magor[2] and was renamed Eveready Industries Ltd (EIIL). Thereafter flashlights and packaged tea were brought under the Eveready brand. Under the leadership of the Khaitans, Eveready underwent many phases of growth. EIIL had the license for the Eveready brand only in India, Bhutan and Nepal from Energizer Holdings, so it had to create a new brand for export to other markets where Energizer Holdings were holding the rights to the Eveready brand. The brand LAVA was launched in 1999. LAVA batteries and flashlights went on to be sold in many countries of Asia and Africa.

In order to increase its domestic market share in India, Eveready acquired the battery business of BPL Energy Systems Ltd (BPL) in 2005 and renamed it as Powercell Batteries. The Powercell portfolio manufactured two brands—BPL Power Cell and BPL Shakti, which enjoyed a combined market share of 8 percent.

To strengthen its position, Eveready forayed into the home care segment by launching mosquito repellents (coils and vaporizers) under the brand Poweron. It leveraged on its brand power and nationwide distribution network to market the products. Over the years, Eveready Industries grew steadily in its business in the battery and tea segments. The company went on to become the largest manufacturer of dry cell batteries in India.

Since 2006, Eveready's batteries and flashlights took a severe beating with low-priced Chinese products dominating the market. The sale of the company's popular brass torch fell from 7 million to 4 million units, plastic flashlights sales fell from 5 million to 2 million.

Table 6.3 Performance of Eveready 2004–2008 (in crore of INR)

	FY04–05	FY05–06	FY06–07	FY07–08
Sales	745.71	827.16	873.87	847.18
Total expenses	588.95	697.77	685.67	784.90
Operating profit	82.12	90.50	45.65	75.30
Net profit	46.31	79.66	(13.43)	(19.32)
EPS (earnings per share)	8.30	11.10	(1.85)	(2.66)

Source: Directors report (from FY04–05–FY07–08). Retrieved from
www.evereadyindustries.com

In 2006–2007, the company posted a loss of Rs 13.43 crore (Rs 0.13 billion) on revenues of Rs 873.87 crore (Rs 8.74 billion) (see Table 6.3). The entry of imported LED torches also killed a good part of the demand for Eveready's D-sized (larger) batteries used in conventional high-powered flashlights. Finally the company launched its first LED torches in December 2006 and followed this up with the launch of LED brass torches.

The dry cell battery—industry size and structure[3]

The Indian dry cell battery market is estimated to be about 2.2 billion pieces in volume and about Rs 14 billion by value. The battery market has only a few players out of which Eveready's market share is about 51 percent (Eveready and Power Cell brands combined). It is the market leader in the dry cell category. Dry cell batteries are of three types—zinc, alkaline and rechargeable. Eveready is one of the world's largest producers of carbon zinc batteries, selling more than 1 billion batteries every year. Other major players include Nippo Batteries, Panasonic India and Geep Batteries. Rapid advances in technology post-1990 flooded the market with portable devices like cameras, toys, scanners, etc. which led to the increase in demand for small-sized UM3 batteries. The demand for batteries, which has been fueled by an increase in the usage of small pocket radios and high powered cameras, had improved dramatically. The shift, in the nature of demand (from D-size batteries to pencil size batteries) has also caused a drastic change in the demand pattern. Consumers shifted to the AA category which is used in many applications of toys, video games, remote controls, etc. The share of the market in terms of various categories and Eveready's share in that market is shown in Table 6.4.

The split of technology in the dry cell market remained constant in the last three years with carbon zinc batteries occupying 97 percent

Table 6.4 The dry cell battery market in India

Battery category	2007–2008		2008–2009		2009–2010	
	Category market share (%)	Eveready's category market share (%)	Category market share (%)	Eveready's category market share (%)	Category market share (%)	Eveready's category market share (%)
D	32.9	34	28.7	31.9	25	27
C	0.7	0.6	0.7	0.6	0.5	1
AA	61.7	61	65.1	61.3	67.3	66
AAA	4.7	4.3	5.5	6.2	7.2	6
	100		100		100	

Source: Directors reports (2007–2008,2008–2009,2009–2010). Retrieved from www. evereadyindustries.com

share of the market. The alkaline batteries have a market share of about 2 percent and are more focused on urban outlets. Rechargeable batteries which have about 1 percent of the market have largely remained stagnant. Consumption of batteries is largely driven by the off take of its applications. The growing need for portable power and the advent of a number of battery operated gadgets catalyze consumption. Since it involves everyday use, demand for batteries is non-cyclical in nature. The alkaline segment in India was dominated by the global brands: Duracell and Energizer. With the acquisition of BPL Energy Systems Ltd, the overall market share of Eveready Industries in the dry cell battery segment was 56 percent in 2005.

Usage

* Incandescent lamps and fluorescent lamps are generally used for indoor lighting. Incandescent lamps are inefficient and have a low shelf life.
* Discharge lamps are energy efficient and have a longer life span. Discharge lamps such as high pressure mercury, high pressure sodium and metal halide are commonly used for outdoor lighting.

Kerosene lamps[4]

As of now, there are around 1.5 billion people in the world without access to the electricity grid, out of which the share of India is about 400 million people. This translates to approximately 100 million families. The majority of them live in the 80,000 or so non-grid connected villages in India. They all depend mainly on kerosene lanterns as the source of light. That makes kerosene a very sensitive commodity in India. Kerosene is sold as a subsidized fuel in government run ration shops for the poor people. Currently it is sold for around Rs 12.50 per liter, but the government gives around Rs 19.60 as a subsidy on top of that to meet the actual open market price of around Rs 32.00. Poor families are eligible to get around 6 liters per month at this subsidized rate.

Kerosene lamp efficiency[5]

As per the study conducted by Lawrence Berkeley National Laboratories in 2003, the energy consumption and light output of kerosene lamps vary a lot. In fact, a lot of kerosene is evaporated through the wick without getting burnt. Typical kerosene lanterns use around 5 ml to 42 ml of kerosene per hour, whereas light outputs vary from around 8 lumens to 67 lumens. This corresponds to light efficiency of 935 lumen hour/liter to 1,914 lumen hour/liter. This leads to an energy efficiency of just 0.1 to 0.2 lumen/watts.

As a comparison, even an average incandescent lamp which many countries want to ban is more than 50 times better than these kerosene lamps. To put it better, kerosene lamps are the costliest and dirtiest way to generate the same light output. Apart from wastage of fuel, other problems like smoke, safety, burning hazard, pollution, etc. are associated with kerosene lamps.

Performance review (2006–2008)

Despite being a player with strong brand equity and better distribution strengths, Eveready suffered its first-ever loss in 2006. In 2006, the Indian market was flooded with LED torches and batteries mainly by Chinese players. The Chinese LED torches were superiorly designed to consume only about one-sixth of the battery power as compared to the incandescent bulb torches sold by most of the Indian players, including Eveready. These long lasting Chinese batteries soon became the customers' preferred choice mainly at the lower end of the market. This adversely affected the sales of Eveready's largest selling D-size batteries. Its sales dropped from 600 million to 300 million units per annum in 2007 in this category. Like a double-edged sword, Eveready's digi LED torches, which consumed less power also, had a negative impact on the company's business since these batteries lasted for a longer period thus impacting repeat sales. From a domestic market leader Eveready saw its position tumbling during 2006 and 2007 (refer to Table 6.3 for the financial results). The shortfall in domestic sales could not be nullified by exports for two reasons. First, Eveready can only sell its products in India, Nepal and Bhutan, as the brand was owned by Energizer in other parts of the world. Second, though Eveready exports small numbers under the LAVA brand, demand for carbon zinc batteries was mostly on the decline in most parts of the world. Alkaline batteries accounted for over 90 percent of the entire demand in major developed countries; however, its share in India was under 2 percent.

The idea behind the experiment

Necessity: The mother of invention

Mr. Partha Biswas, Strategic Business Unit Head of Batteries recalled while discussing with the case writer, "We had to hit upon a fast idea of bolstering the demand for the dry cells." The entire top management understood the fact that it was one of the most disruptive phases in the history of Eveready Industries. Mr. Biswas emphatically recalled, "the brief given to us by Mr. Khaitan was to think radically about usages of dry cells in different applications that can create a new market." Mr. Khaitan's apprehension forced him into devising a strategy that would bolster his company's sagging fortunes, and suddenly he found inspiration from Eveready's history. Recalling the fact that way back in 1958, Union Carbide had made a forward integration into torch manufacturing by starting a plant in Lucknow to boost the sale of the batteries Mr. Khaitan wondered "could there be a significantly large application of dry cell batteries for solving the mundane needs of society?" Several questions were simultaneously running in his mind. Could Eveready address certain requirements of society which can be primarily targeted at the bottom-of-pyramid customer? Could Eveready develop a product at the right price, which could transform the company? What were the strengths Eveready already had that could be leveraged to build new businesses?

Mr. Biswas recalls there were many brain-storming sessions with senior management. It all started with a one point agenda of finding a product which could be highly value enhancing and at the same time be cost effective. Also the product had to cater to a mass market that would benefit a large section of society. Mr. Khaitan had mentioned that the company was sitting on a huge opportunity with endless possibilities. Could it really come up with something special during this hour of adversity and convert it into an opportunity? Biswas specifically mentions that top management had left them with a thought: "Can Eveready regenerate as a company and revitalize itself?" Thereafter at every meeting that top management had with SBU heads and the product development teams, it basically tried to address what could be the big idea that could be transformational and not incremental. Could its competency be used as leverage to create a new product? Could the combination of LED, torch, lantern, battery, backed up with cost effectiveness, safety, reliability and durability be configured to create a new product?

The team gathered at one such meeting in late 2008 and tried to relate the fact that Eveready represented a company which basically was trying to find an alternative usage of light. Was there an opportunity in terms of catering to certain customers who are deprived of electric power in the first place? Is this a fundamental need in an emerging country like India where more than 70 percent of people lived in villages and many states are deprived of electricity? Even in areas where electricity is available, the supply is too erratic. Could Eveready come up with a partial solution to this problem and in the process leverage its own strengths? Ultimately it dawned upon the team to identify a proposition in the form of an LED lamp that was worth experimenting with. On further deliberations it was felt that an LED lantern held an enormous proposition in an emerging country like India. Mr. Khaitan then asked the task force to develop this idea further with the brief: "To come up with a light which lasts for a month and is cheaper than kerosene lamps." In about a week's time they came back with an idea—to develop a lamp (lantern) for the rural market specifically that can substitute a traditional kerosene lamp. However, the team questioned itself on the proposition—why would a poor person in a rural area try out something new unless it is cost effective?

Mr. Biswas mentioned that the challenge before them was to create a lamp that would substitute a kerosene lamp. How could they configure the product cost effectively? Mr. Biswas and his team tried contacting suppliers in China who could do that. After Mr. Khaitan was briefed on the feasibility aspect and the supply chain, he was convinced that the idea was indeed viable. The task force further reported that based on test reports carried out by the product development team the idea was feasible. Further test reports showed it was possible to design a lantern that could offer better lighting to consumers, at a price marginally less than the cost to operate a kerosene lamp. Besides, LED lamps offered better reliability, the safety option and with no precursor of setting up the lamp every time as is the case with a kerosene lamp. Added to this aspect was the fact that it was environmentally friendly, as no smoke or soot was generated as a byproduct, unlike a kerosene lamp. The last clincher—LED lamps would require no service at all. That is how the LED lamp was conceived.

The magic lamp: Business model innovation?

Was it a simple but brilliant idea after all? Mr. Biswas explained the rationale for the experimental foray. The product if designed well could be marketed to consumers in traditional power-starved states like UP, Bihar, West Bengal, Jharkhand, Assam, etc.: (a) in many of these states availability of electric power is sometimes as low as 12 hours per day. It could be marketed even in states where electric power existed but the frequent load sheddings made people suffer; (b) as the LED lamp would require batteries for it to operate, it would create a significant traction for the company's battery business.

The launch

The product development team further did a cost–benefit analysis to understand the value proposition for the prospective buyers:

1. It demonstrated that with one set of batteries inside the lamp, the cost works out to be about 50 paise (an equivalent of 1 INR is 100 paise) compared to 58 paise for kerosene lamps. It made a very viable proposition on the part of Eveready to go ahead.
2. On the issue of benefit to the customers, the product development team found that the advantages of the LED lamp over the kerosene lamp were multifold. (See Table 6.5 for details.) Continuous bright white light compared to a flickering white yellow light of a kerosene lamp.

    *   Easy and safe to operate
    *   No risk of fire compared to kerosene lamps where the flame is exposed
    *   Smoke free and maintenance free compared to kerosene lamps
    *   Durability of LED is much higher
    *   No toxic fumes, black soot and unpleasant odor

3. The D-size batteries of Eveready could be used in the LED lamps to boost the sale of the existing battery business.

With all these facts and insights, Mr. Khaitan and his team were convinced about this idea. They went to meet potential suppliers in China for finalization of components and parts of the lamp. Thus began the developmental work of an experimental idea and history repeated itself at the same plant 50 years hence. Mr. Khaitan candidly said about

Table 6.5 Advantages of Eveready Home LITE over kerosene lamp/candle

Kerosene lamp/candle	*Eveready Home LITE*
Flickering white yellow light	Continuous bright white light
Flame is exposed	Anti-glare arrangement of LEDs
Difficult to operate	Push button, easy and safe to operate
Fragile, weak handle	Dual handle, easy to carry and hang
Glass body, breaks easily, melts away creating mess around	Long lasting ABS plastic body
Risk of fire	No risk of fire
Emits toxic fumes	Smoke free light
Emits black soot and unpleasant odor	Maintenance free light
Body heats up when lit	Heat resistant body
Wick needs to be replaced regularly	Long lasting LEDs—does not fuse
Requires regular refills of kerosene oil, candles require replacement	No recharging required. The 3 D-size batteries give light for 80 hours (intermittent use of 2–3 hours a day)

Source: *Hexagon*, November 2009 (company in-house newsletter)

the Chinese products, "We copied LED for torches initially. They made us learn more about LED." He was emphatic in saying, "The test results show that at 2–3 hours of usage every day, the LED lanterns cost 50 paise an hour, which is marginally lower than the cost to operate kerosene lanterns." While the idea was being conceived, the advantages of LED lamps were highlighted prominently in their in-house newsletter, *Hexagon*, November 2009 issue. The value proposition of the LED lantern hinged around better light at lower cost (refer to Table 6.5). Eveready did some advertisements in leading regional dailies with this message before even assessing how many they could sell initially and what capacity of production to start off with. Mr. Khaitan immediately commissioned the manufacturing of the HL08 model to begin with and production started in February 2009 directly after the key components of the LED lantern were made available in-house. The HL08 model used a plastic body, gave a superior white light and made use of three D-size batteries.

Initial response

LED lanterns have sold more than 3 million units since April 2009, gaining significant traction in power deficient states such as Uttar Pradesh, Bihar, West Bengal and Assam. In April 2009, Eveready sold 20,000 lanterns, in May 40,000 and in June 60,000 units. But as soon as advertisements came out in the second week of July 2009, sales

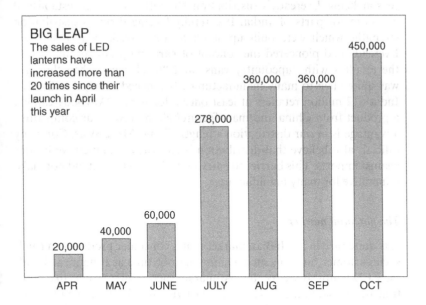

BIG LEAP
The sales of LED lanterns have increased more than 20 times since their launch in April this year

Figure 6.3 Initial response
Source: *Business World*, November 27, 2009

went up to 278,000 and the company was virtually out of stock. In the three months since then, sales have averaged 400,000 to 450,000 units a month which could have been more if not for the manufacturing capacity constraints (see Figure 6.3).

In terms of contribution from sales of LED lamps, the turnover of Rs 3.82 crore (Rs 38.2 million) achieved in 2008–2009, zoomed to Rs 50 crore (Rs 500 million) in 2009–2010. In terms of top line growth, revenues at Eveready went up by nearly 20 percent in the third quarter of 2009. (Refer to Table 6.5 for details.) "I can sell 500,000 a month if I could produce them," remarked Mr. Khaitan who then set a stiffer target to sell 1 million units a month beginning fiscal year 2010–2011 when his capacity constraints would be taken care of. It is not out of place to mention in all fairness that local players discovered the power of LED lanterns well before Eveready—a few priced between Rs 50 and Rs 200 in the market. However, no player could capitalize on this huge opportunity the way Eveready did, for two reasons. The first reason was that no player scaled up manufacturing capacity. The small time fringe players were too small to move from one market to another without proper manufacturing capacities in place. The other reason being Eveready's distribution strengths were well established across major parts of India. It carefully leveraged on its distribution strengths which were built up about 50 years back. Way back then Eveready had pioneered the concept of carrying products right up to the retailers with "upcountry vans" and "local vans" when this idea was quite alien to many manufacturers. It touched nearly 4 million of India's 12 million retailers at least once a fortnight. "Anybody can get a product from China and manufacture/sell, however, our competitive advantage is in our distribution strengths," said Mr. Biswas. Company officials also believe that distribution is Eveready's competitive barrier against imports. This barrier to entry in the Indian market did not make it lucrative for many manufacturers.

The potential market

It is quite rare in the Indian market that a consumer product can catch such customer fancy in such a short span of time as it happened with the LED lamps. If we recall mass-market successful products like radio transistors sold in India every year, the figure is only about 6 million per year. This goes to prove how successful the product was and the potential it holds for the markets that Eveready has targeted. To realize this potential, Eveready hoped to tap nearly 100,000 villages that are still not on India's power map. Company officials mention there are at least 200,000 villages which have power but the supply is too irregular to call it a supply. Mr. Khaitan estimated that the total number of households to whom he can sell at least one LED lantern could be as high as 350 million. This translates to potential business worth Rs 10,500 crore (around $2.2 billion or nearly 11 times his company's current turnover in 2009–2010).

The product portfolio

The Eveready LED lanterns portfolio has grown to nine since April 2009, priced between Rs 150 and Rs 450. But Mr. Khaitan is now desperate to prevent competition from capitalizing on his success. The range will be bolstered to 20 by 2010–2011 to target at every price point in the portfolio. New offerings would include mass-market products such as a detachable lamp that can be fixed on a bicycle and niche products such as a headlamp for miners, doctors or hikers.

Analysts feel the company will need to improve its financials and product development capability significantly for greater investor interest. In fiscal year 2008–2009, for instance, Eveready reported a net profit of

Table 6.6 The LED lamps have boosted Eveready's quarterly income (figures in crore of INR)

	Sept. 2008	Dec. 2008	Mar. 2009	June 2009	Sept. 2009
Sales	219.99	214.93	205.73	232.86	263.34
Total expenses	200.52	192.90	187.15	203.05	229.02
Operating profit	19.47	22.03	18.58	29.81	34.32
Net profit	2.26	8.43	5.59	16.05	17.54
EPS (in Rs)	0.31	1.16	0.77	2.21	2.41

Source: Directors report (from FY04–05 to FY07–08). Retrieved from www.evereadyindustries.com

Table 6.7 Financial performance in 2008–2009 and 2009–2010

	2008–2009	2009–2010
Net sales	857.33	968.73
Total income	860.49	977.18
Expenses	778.83	852.05
Operating profit	83.61	125.13
Net profit	19.40	44.84*

*excluding exceptional items (figures in crore of INR).

Source: Annual reports 2008–2009 and 2009–2010

19.40 crore (Rs 0.194 billion) on sales turnover of 860 crore (Rs 8.6 billion) (see Table 6.6). In comparison, its nearest rival Nippo Batteries (Lakhanpal National Ltd) posted a net profit of Rs 16 crore (on a turn-over of Rs 307.51 crore (Rs 3.075 billion). "Our operating margins are slowly moving up. We intend to take it from the existing 13 percent of the turnover to around 18 percent in the next two years," Mr. Khaitan said in 2009. While quarterly net profit ranged from Rs 2 to 8.5 crore (Rs 0.02 to Rs .085 billion)in the preceding three-quarters, it has more than doubled the net profit to 16.05 and 17.54 crore (Rs 0.16 billion and Rs 0.175 billion) in June and September quarters of 2009 (see Table 6.7).

The challenges

Beyond the successful launch of the LED lanterns, there are huge risks and challenges Mr. Khaitan faces. The challenges began with the prop-osition of introducing "rechargeable lanterns" as many customers are enquiring about them. But the industry, as well as Eveready, is still guessing whether the rechargeable lantern market will ever be as strong as single-life battery lanterns. If Mr. Khaitan does introduce them, they defeat the very purpose for which he set up his lanterns business—to prop up D-size battery sales. If he does not—and a rival introduces a better value proposition—Eveready's nascent lanterns business could be severely hit.

As a part of company strategy, Eveready has attacked the "costly" rechargeable lanterns in a provocative campaign suggesting consumers must buy four single-life battery lanterns for the price of a rechargeable lantern. Mr. Partha Biswas, SBU head has a more fundamental question to ask: "In many parts of rural India, there is no power. Bihar and Uttar Pradesh go through power cuts of 12–15 hours a day. How will you recharge?" When asked about the proposition of introducing solar lanterns, Mr. Khaitan said: "As a company, why would I encourage selling solar? It will cannibalize my offerings and cut down my battery consumption." Besides, Eveready sees itself as a mass-market FMCG company and any product which does not sell more than 100,000 pieces per month is not worthwhile for it to take up. As competition intensifies from other local players with the onset of winter, Eveready is faced with a peculiar challenge: The sales of kerosene lamp sales peak in north and east India during winters because families use them as a source of heat as much as light. Mr. Khaitan's biggest challenge as of now is to ensure that he generates enough heat with his offerings to keep his portfolio trendy and relevant.

Notes

1   Earlier published by Swarup Kumar Dutta (2014) Eveready Industries: The magic lamp that changed the fortunes. Asian Case Research Journal, 18(1), 1–34. Reproduced with permission.
2   www.sify.com/.../kit-the-indian-dry-cell-market-newsdefault-kiqbkE
3   www.sify.com/.../kit-the-indian-dry-cell-market-newsdefault-kiqbkE
4   This section is based on Mills (2003).
5   This section is based on Mills (2003).

References

Dubey, R. (2009, December 7). Deepak Khaitan and his magic Lamp. *Business World*, pp. 42–46.
Mills, E. (2003, June 28). *Technical and economic performance analysis of kerosene lamps and alternative approaches to illumination in developing countries* (Report). Berkeley, CA: University of California: Lawrence Berkeley National Laboratory.

Author index

Subject index

9781032931203